MARGARET SANDBACH

Trasiedi mewn Inc a Marmor ~ A Tragedy in Marble & Ink

Cyhoeddwyd gyntaf ym Mhrydain Fawr yn 2013 gan Ymddiriedolaeth Cadwraeth Castell Gwrych/Gwasg Gwrych

Ar gael Hydref 2013

© Ymddiriedolaeth Cadwraeth Castell Gwrych

www.margaretsandbach.co.uk

Ariannwyd gan Bartneriaeth Wledig Conwy, Cadw a Chyngor Celfyddydau Cymru

Cynlluniwyd gan Washington Design

Argraffwyd gan Stephens & George Print Group

ISBN: 978-0-9927241-0-8

First published in Great Britain in 2013 by Gwrych Castle Preservation Trust/Gwasg Gwrych

Released October 2013

© Gwrych Castle Preservation Trust

www.margaretsandbach.co.uk

Funded by Conwy Rural Partnership, Cadw and Arts Council Wales

Designed by Washington Design

Printed by Stephens & George Print Group

ISBN: 978-0-9927241-0-8

IN MEMORIAM

Ian Mackeson-Sandbach
1933-2012

Contents / Cynnwys

Rhagair

Gall olrhain hanes teulu unrhyw un greu peth teimlad o anesmwythyd a chwithdod, a phan gysylltodd yr awduron â mi i ddweud ei bod am ymchwilio i fywyd Margaret Sandbach, fy ymateb cyntaf oedd pam? Mae'r hanes pwerus a theimladwy hwn o fywyd Margaret yn croniclo ei hangerdd at Ogledd Cymru a'r dylanwad gafodd hi ar bawb o'i chwmpas. Roedd ganddi'r un diddordebau â phob gwraig fonheddig arall yng nghyfnod Fictoria, er hynny, gall rhywun ond meddwl pe ganed hi mewn cyfnod mwy diweddar y byddai rhagor o bwys wedi'i roi ar ei cherddi. Arweiniodd y profiadau gafodd ar y Daith Fawr ym 1838 a 1839 at gyfeillgarwch oes â'r cerflunydd Gibson yn ogystal â chael effaith dyngedfennol ar ei gweithiau llenyddol.

Wedi iddi hi gyhoeddi Giuliano de Medici-A Drama-with Other Poems cafodd y gyfrol dderbyniad cymysg, a chyhoeddodd Margaret weddill ei llyfrau'n ddienw a chawsant dderbyniad gwell. Efallai bod hyn yn enghraifft o'r ffiniau roedd gofyn i ferched y cyfnod eu goresgyn. Fodd bynnag, mae ei dylanwad yn parhau hyd heddiw, drwy ei chyfeillgarwch dwfn â'r cerflunydd Gibson a'r ffaith i'w cyfeillgarwch ysbrydoli y cerfluniau a'r cerddi oedd yn cydgerdded law yn llaw.

I mi mae gweld a chlywed Margaret a Henry yn disgrifio eu bywyd a'r wlad o amgylch Hafodunos yn deimlad hynod arbennig, mae'r gwrychoedd â'u blagur a'r golygfeydd dros y wlad hyfryd yn parhau. Mae eu hagosatrwydd yn llamu o'r tudalennau ac mae'n deimladwy tu hwnt. Yng ngeiriau Margaret ei hun:'When I look at my dearest Harry and think, I may stay yet a little longer with him, the hope is too fond, too precious, to dwell upon it, and under the resignation I

Foreword

Delving into the past of one's family is always something that is done with a hint of trepidation, and when the authors approached me to say that he was looking into the life of Margaret Sandbach, my initial reaction was why? This powerful and moving story of Margaret's life chronicles Margaret's lifelong love of North Wales and the impression she made on those around her. Her pursuits were similar to many Victorian ladies of the era, however one can't help having the feeling that had she been born in more modern times, that Margaret's poetry would have been taken much more seriously. The effect of the Grant Tour in 1838 and 1839, leading to a lifelong friendship with sculptor Gibson, as well as having a momentous impact on Margaret's own writings.

After releasing Giuliano de Medici-A Drama-with Other Poems to a mixed critical reception, Margaret went on to release further books anonymously, to much more favourable reviews. This is perhaps symptomatic of the barriers that women living at that time had to overcome. However Margaret continues to have an impact, even today, because of her deep friendship with the sculptor Gibson and the fact that their friendship provided a source of inspiration with the sculpture and poetry often walking hand in hand.

For me seeing and hearing Margaret and Henry describing through their diaries the life and landscape around Hafodunos, is immensely special, the bursting hedgerows and verdant green landscape remains. The closeness of their personal relationship together leaps from the pages, and is deeply touching. Margaret writes 'When I look at my dearest Harry and think, I may stay yet a little longer with him, the hope is too fond, too

Hafodunos, by a member of the Williams Family of Bryngwyn, circa 1860.
Private Collection.

Hafodunos gan aelod o'r teulu Williams, Bryngwyn, tua 1860. Casgliad Preifat.

precious, to dwell upon it, and under the resignation I have been able to attain to - a week ago all was complete anxiety and complete hopelessness, it is the past week that has brought better symptoms – therefore they seem brighter for being unexpected.'

The contrast between the earlier diary entries which show Margaret as a chatty and humorous correspondent, and the later slow chronicle of disease and death, is something that anyone whose family has been affected by cancer will recognise. The tragedy of her demise at forty is reflected in her poetry as she struggles to deal with her approaching death. The authors weave the life of Margaret with her poetry, her friendship with Gibson and the backdrop of Victorian life into a readable colourful tapestry which chronicles both success and tragedy.

Antoinette Sandbach AM

have been able to attain to - a week ago all was complete anxiety and complete hopelessness, it is the past week that has brought better symptoms – therefore they seem brighter for being unexpected.'

Bydd y cyferbyniad rhwng y dyddiaduron cynnar sy'n darlunio Margaret fel person oedd yn hoff o gynnal sgwrs ac yn llawn hwyl, a'r cofnod diweddaraf o afiechyd a thranc, yn gyffredin i unrhyw un sydd â theulu wedi'i effeithio gan ganser. Adlewyrchir trasiedi ei marwolaeth yn ddeugain oed yn ei cherddi wrth iddi geisio cynefino â'i marwolaeth agos. Llwyddodd yr awduron i weu bywyd Margaret a'i cherddi, ei chyfeillgarwch â Gibson a chefndir bywyd yn y cyfnod Fictoraidd yn un tapestri lliwgar sy'n rhwydd ei ddarllen ac sy'n gofnod o lwyddiant a thrasiedi.

Antoinette Sandbach AC

Arwres goll o gyfnod y frenhines Fictoria yw Margaret Sandbach(1812-1852). Swynwyd Henry Robertson Sandbach (1809-1895), llanc ifanc a ddaeth yn ŵr iddi, a John Gibson (1790-1866), prif gerflunydd ei oes, gan ei hysbryd creadigol a di-ildio. Cynhyrchwyd rhai o gerfluniau enwocaf y cyfnod hwnnw gan John Gibson.

Roedd Margaret yn berson o allu arbennig, a chofnodwyd ei bywyd cymharol fyr drwy ei gweithiau llenyddol niferus a'i nawdd artistig. Yn ei chyfrolau barddoniaeth, ei llythyrau a'i dyddiaduron hi, rhai ei gŵr a Gibson, mae stori gymhleth ac enbyd o ramant, nawdd a gofid, oll yn ei chartref boneddigaidd yn Hafodunos, Llangernyw, Gogledd Cymru.

Fe'i ganed ar 28 Ebrill 1812 yn Garden Lodge, Lerpwl. Hi oedd ail blentyn ac unig ferch Edward Roscoe (1785-1834) a Margaret Lace (1786/7-1840). Roedd Margaret yn boenus o ymwybodol o'i marwoldeb drwy gydol ei hoes fer. Daethpwyd o hyd iddi, yn blentyn ifanc, yn cysgu gyda chorff ei brawd marw, a daeth y berthynas rhwng brawd a chwaer yn nodwedd arbennig o'i gwaith. Cyfeiriodd Gibson, hyd yn oed, ati fel 'Darling Sis' drwy gydol eu cyfeillgarwch a'u llythyrau toreithiog. Ym 1832, priododd â Henry Robertson Sandbach oedd yn etifedd i gyfoeth cwmni masnachol y teulu Sandbach.

Entrepreneur oedd Samuel Sandbach (1769-1851), tad Henry, a daeth yn ŵr goludog iawn drwy ei ddawn mewn busnes. Sefydlwyd Sandbach, Tinne & Co. ym 1782 yn Demerara gan James McInroy.

Margaret Sandbach (1812-1852) is a lost heroine of the Victorian age whose indomitable creative spirit enchanted both her husband, the young Henry Robertson Sandbach (1809-1895), and the master sculptor of the time, John Gibson (1790-1866), who produced some of the most celebrated sculpture of the age.

Margaret was a woman of remarkable ability, whose relatively fleeting life is preserved through her extensive writing and artistic patronage. The several volumes of poems she produced, together with her letters and diaries, and those of her husband and Gibson, reveal a complex and tragic story of love, patronage and grief in the genteel surroundings of her home, Hafodunos, in Llangernyw, North Wales.

Born on 28th April 1812 at Garden Lodge in Liverpool, Margaret was the second child and only daughter of Edward Roscoe (1785-1834) and Margaret Lace (1786/7-1840). Throughout her short life Margaret was painfully aware of her own mortality. She was found as an infant, sleeping with the body of her dead brother and the relationship between siblings became a marked feature of her work. Even Gibson referred to Margaret as 'Darling Sis' throughout their friendship in their extensive correspondence. In 1832, she married the heir to the Sandbach mercantile fortune, Henry Robertson Sandbach.

His father, Samuel Sandbach (1769-1851), was an entrepreneur, whose business talents made him a very rich man. Sandbach, Tinne & Co. was founded in 1782 in Demerara by James McInroy.

[1] Margaret Sandbach, 'Dulcibel', Aurora and other poems, (London: Pickering, 1850), pp.124-5.

Dulcibel

DULCIBEL is singing low,
And her steps are soft and slow;
Softly, carefully they go,
Voice and step together.
Off her brow the shining hair
Is thrown away; and pale and fair,
Parted locks, and forehead bare,
Woo the wind and weather.
Dulcibel is loved and blest;
Singing she smiles, and is at rest,
Nursing in her gentle breast,
Love and Peace together.
Innocent is Dulcibel
Of all beside; but she can tell,
That her loving God doth dwell
In yon Heaven above her.
Silver mist of summer morn,
Veiled the Earth when she was born;
And her life the cloud has worn, —
A soft transparent shadow.
Like a wandering, wondering child,
She glides along; holy and mild,
Breathing sweet words and music wild, —
Dulcibel, the dreamer.[2]

Aurora, the winged goddess of the dawn, holding an amphora in each
hand, with waves below her feet, illustration to The Art Journal, 1849.
Stipple and engraving. British Museum.

Aurora, duwies asgellog y wawr, yn gafael mewn amffora yn ei dwy
law, a thonnau dan ei thraed. Darlun ar gyfer The Art Journal, 1849.
Dotwaith ac ysgythriad. Yr Amgueddfa Brydeinig.

[2]Margaret Sandbach, 'Dulcibel', Aurora and other poems, (London: Pickering, 1850), pp.124-5.

Roeddent yn berchnogion llongau, delwyr mewn nwyddau, masnachwyr ac yn berchnogion ar blanhigfeydd ac yn allforio siwgr, coffi, triagl, rỳm a chaethweision o India'r Gorllewin. Ymwelodd Samuel â Grenada a Demerara ym 1789, ac ym 1790 ymunodd â chwmni McInroy gyda Charles Stuart Parker a George Robertson gan greu'r cwmni McInroy, Sandbach & Co. Dychwelodd Sandbach i Lerpwl ym 1801 ac yno bu pencadlys y cwmni o 1813 hyd at Rhagfyr 1892. Roedd Samuel yn faer Lerpwl ym 1831-2, ac ymddeolodd o'r cwmni Sandbach, Tinne & Co ym 1833 wedi iddo brynu Hafodunos. Daeth yn Uchel-Siryf Sir Ddinbych ym 1839, er nad Hafodunos oedd ei brif breswylfa.

Yn ystod ei thaith fawr yn Ewrop, cyfarfu Margaret â John Gibson yn ei stiwdio yn Rhufain. Cynnwyd fflam carwriaeth blatonig rhyngddynt oedd i barhau weddill eu hoes. Roedd celfyddyd y naill yn ysbrydoli'r llall: barddoni Margaret a cherflunio Gibson. Mae eu llythyrau, dyddiaduron a ffrwyth eu celfyddyd yn dyst i'w perthynas angerddol a chreadigol. Gadawsant ar eu hôl etifeddiaeth barhaol ym myd llenyddiaeth a chelfyddyd. Yn ei thri degau, yn ei chartref paradwysaidd yn Hafodunos, dechreuodd Margaret frwydro yn erbyn canser y fron. Cafodd lawdriniaeth arloesol yn Llundain i godi'i bron a thriniaethau ar sawl tyfiant arall, gyda chloroffform ar adegau, hebddo bryd arall - fel mae ei dyddiaduron yn ei iasol ddatgelu. Hafodunos oedd ei noddfa, ei hysbrydoliaeth i ysgrifennu, a'r man lle casglodd y nifer mwyaf o gerfluniau Gibson drwy Ewrop gyfan. Denwyd yno awduron ac artistiaid o bell ac agos.

Yn y llythyrau rhwng Margaret a Gibson gwelir sut y bu hi o gymorth iddo ddewis ei destunau a sut y cafodd ei ysbrydoli gan ei dewrder. Cafodd hithau, yn ei thro, ei hysbrydoli i ysgrifennu ei chyfrol olaf o farddoniaeth, a gyflwynwyd i Gibson, gan ei gwaith comisiwn mwyaf

They were ship-owners, produce brokers, general merchants and plantation owners. Exporting coffee, molasses, rum and also Coolies from the West Indies. Samuel visited Grenada and Demerara in 1789 and by 1790 he joined McInroy's company with Charles Stewart Parker and George Robertson, forming the company, McInroy, Sandbach & Co. Sandbach returned to Liverpool in 1801 and the company's headquarters was based in Liverpool from 1813 to December 31st 1892. Samuel was the mayor of Liverpool in 1831-2, and retired from his position at Sandbach, Tinne & Co. in 1833 after purchasing Hafodunos. He later became the High Sheriff of Denbighshire in 1839, even though Hafodunos was not his main residence.

Whilst on a grand tour of continental Europe, Margaret met John Gibson at his studio in Rome. This meeting sparked a platonic love affair that was to last the rest of their lives. Each one's art inspired the other's: Margaret's poetry, and Gibson's sculpture. Their letters, diaries and works of art chronicle an intensely creative relationship and have left a lasting literary and sculptural legacy. During her thirties, Margaret fought the onset of breast cancer in the idyllic surroundings of Hafodunos. Margaret's journal chillingly reveals she underwent surgery in London and a pioneering mastectomy; further lumpectomies endured with chloroform, sometimes without. Hafodunos was her escape from life; it inspired her writings and was where she amassed the largest repository of Gibson's art in Europe, attracting writers and artists from far afield.

Letters to and from Margaret reveal how she helped Gibson choose his subjects; how her bravery inspired him; and how her major commission, Aurora (now in the National Museum of Wales, Cardiff) inspired her in turn to write her last collection of poetry, which she dedicated to him. After much suffering, she passed away at Hafodunos at the age of forty, leaving a grieving husband and a desolate Gibson. Margaret's image was to feature often in Gibson's subsequent work and he designed, with Sir George Gilbert Scott, a sculpture gallery at Hafodunos in her memory.

Margaret passed away before she could finish her memoirs. However, in this final work, she considered the value of autobiography:

iddo, Aurora (sydd bellach yn Amgueddfa Genedlaethol Cymru). Wedi mawr ddioddef, bu hi farw yn Hafodunos yn ddeugain mlwydd oed, gan adael gŵr galarus, a Gibson yn amddifad. Mae delwedd Margaret i'w gweld mewn sawl darn o waith gan Gibson wedi hynny, a chyda Syr George Gilbert Scott cynlluniodd oriel gerfluniau yn gofadail iddi hi yn Hafodunos.

Bu farw Margaret cyn cwblhau ei chofiannau. Er hynny, yn ei gwaith olaf, mae hi'n ystyried gwerth ei hunangofiant:

John Gibson by J. Severn. One of the first drawings of Gibson in Rome dated 1828 and signed J. Severn. Private Collection.

John Gibson gan J Severn. Un o'r lluniadau cyntaf o Gibson yn Rhufain, dyddiedig 1828, wedi'i arwyddo J Severn. Casgliad Preifat.

I have often thought and heard it remarked by others that the simple record of a thoughtful life, truthfully told, whether its outward aspect be calm or troubled, marked by stirring event or flowing in placid evenings, could not fail to be interesting, if only from the very circumstances of its truthfulness and individuality. The feelings that have been really felt, the hopes that have throbbed in a living breast, the love that has brightened a path that we ourselves are treading, the faith which has supported a soul – struggling with the very difficulties and doubts which may beset our own – these speak to us – they go straight to our hearts' sympathy and are answered there.

When I have heard people relating the instance, and experience of their childhood, I have been struck with the lesson this experience conveyed; with the strong light thrown upon points of character and education too often left in the shade. Biographies in general aiming at a later time, when the remarkable points in life and character on to be portrayed, 'haps too hastily over this interesting and important period; it may be because so little material is left for a record of the childhood of remarkable men and women, and because being remarkable men and women, the memoir hastens to set forth the things of which the world takes most cognizance. It is true that the most talented and remarkable persons have not exhibited the most interesting traits in childhood – it is not however an intellectual but a moral lesson we should draw from a record of the simplest early life.

The beautiful thoughts that come and go on the pure atmosphere of childhood's life, the intense affections that burn in its little breast, the wonderful intimations of divine love that speak to its humbly inquiring soul, the sharp struggles in the strife of obedience with self will – how little we know of all of them, save from our own experience; how much would have been appeared to others had we known more; how many infant rebukes would have been silenced, how many a harsh glance unexpressed – had the child been better understood![3]

[1] Llandrindod Wells, Powys Record Office, MS M/D/SAND/4/4. This manuscript, entitled 'Record of a Country House' was begun on the 23rd March by Margaret Sandbach and left unfinished during the first week of June 1852, a few weeks before her death.

Dechreuwyd ar y gwaith o ailddarganfod perthynas John Gibson, a Margaret Sandbach fu'n gymaint o ysbrydoliaeth iddo, yn 2002 pan ymwelodd Mark Baker, hanesydd pensaernïol o Gymro, â Hafodunos a oedd bryd hynny'n blasty gwag. Roedd olion bywydau'r tri i'w gweld yno wedi treigl o 150 blynedd. Roedd cerfweddau Gibson yn crogi ar y muriau bregus ac arysgrif coffa Margaret yn amgylchynu ffris yr oriel gerfluniau. Roedd y gerddi yn y cwm bychan, gynlluniwyd gan Margaret o flaen Hafodunos yn llawn lliw a phlanhigion amrywiol, er eu bod wedi tyfu'n wyllt ac anhrefnus. Dechreuwyd ar y gwaith araf a gofalus o ymchwilio ac ail-greu y bywyd, y cariad a'r ing fu yn y tŷ dirgel yma yng Nghymru. Tristwch yw nodi y cynnwyd tân yn fwriadol yn Hafodunos un noson yn 2004 a ddifrodwyd tu mewn yr adeilad.

Adfeilion trawiadol Hafodunos yw cefndir pedwar o'r ffotograffau tablo yn y llyfr hwn. Mae ein diolch yn ddyledus i berchennog y plasty, Rick Wood. Mae'r gyfres o naw ffotograff o waith yr Eidalwr Manuel Vason[4] yn ymateb i agweddau gwahanol o fywyd a gwaith Margaret Sandbach. Bydd arddangosfa deithiol o'r gwaith i'w weld 2014. Mae'r ffotograffiaeth newydd o Hafodunos gan Antonia Dewhurst, sy'n ymwelydd cyson â'r safle.

Hanes bywyd a rhamant Margaret sydd yn y llyfr hwn, a sut yr ysbrydolodd gariad a serch yn y ddau ŵr oedd agosaf ati. Daw cymaint o'r stori â phosibl drwy eu geiriau hwy eu hunain a'u gweithiau creadigol.

The re-discovery of John Gibson's relationship to his muse, Margaret Sandbach, began in 2002 when Mark Baker, a Welsh architectural historian, first visited the then empty mansion of Hafodunos. Reminders of the trio's lives were still evident, despite the passing of 150 years. Gibson's reliefs clung to the crumbling walls of dilapidated rooms and Margaret's memorial inscription encircled the sculpture gallery frieze. The gardens, laid out by Margaret though wild and overgrown, were rich in colour and variety, blanketing the little valley in which Hafodunos sits. A slow, careful journey had begun; researching and reassembling the lives, loves and heartaches of this hidden Welsh house. Sadly, one night in 2004, Hafodunos was set alight by arsonists and its interiors perished.

The spectacular ruins of Hafodunos provide the backdrop for four of the photographic tableaux in this book, thanks to the generosity of its owner, Rick Wood. The series of nine images appear in a touring exhibition in 2014 and were commissioned from Italian photographer Manuel Vason[4] as a response to aspects of Margaret Sandbach's life and work. The new photography of Hafodunos is by Antonia Dewhurst, who is a regular visitor to the site.

This book tells the story of how Margaret lived, loved and inspired the love and affection of the two men closest to her. It is told as much as possible in their own words and through their own art works.

[4]Delweddau Manuel Vason mewn cydweithrediad â Truth Department, gyda chymorth Cyngor Celfyddydau Cymru.
Images by Manuel Vason in a collaboration with Truth Department, with the support of Arts Council of Wales.

I

'Amid those haunts our happy childhood knew…'[1]

Ym 1810, priododd Edward Roscoe ei gyfyrder Margaret Lace (merch Joshua a Margaret Lace) a oedd eisoes yn feichiog â'u plentyn cyntaf, William. Aeth y ddau i fyw i'r Garden Lodge ar dir Allerton Hall, cartref William Roscoe. Symudodd teulu Margaret i Ogledd Cymru tra roedd hi'n blentyn ifanc. Bu ei thad, Edward Roscoe yn gweithio mewn gwaith smeltio plwm ym Magillt, Sir y Fflint ers 1804. Cynyddodd buddiannau'r teulu ym 1809 pan ymgorfforwyd pyllau glo'r Dee Bank, a daeth y teulu Roscoe yn feistri glo llwyddiannus gan allforio glo a phlwm o Gymru drwy borthladd Lerpwl i weddill Prydain a'r byd. Gan fod y cwmni'n ffynnu ac Edward bellach â swydd is-reolwr ers 1812, rhaid oedd i'r teulu fyw yng Ngogledd Cymru. Symudodd y teulu i Pistyll, tŷ Sioraidd ger Treffynnon, ac yma y treuliodd Margaret ei blynyddoedd cynnar gyda'i brodyr, William (1810/11-1815) ac Edward Henry (1813-1866). Cofnododd yn ei chofiant personol:

In 1810 Edward Roscoe married his second cousin, Margaret (daughter of Joshua and Margaret Lace), who was already pregnant with their first child, William. The couple moved into Garden Lodge in the grounds of Allerton Hall, the home of William Roscoe, Edward's father. The Roscoe family relocated during her infancy to North Wales, where her father, Edward Roscoe, had been working at a lead smelting plant near Bagillt, Flintshire, since 1804. The family's business interests were increased in 1809 when Dee Bank collieries were purchased and the Roscoes became successful mine owners, exporting Welsh coal and lead via Liverpool, around Britain and overseas. It was necessary, with the success of the business and Edward becoming under-manager for Dee Bank in 1812, that the family lived in North Wales. Pistyll, a Georgian house near Holywell was chosen and it was here that Margaret spent her formative years with her brothers, William (1810/11-1815) and Edward Henry (1813-1866). She recalled in her unpublished memoirs:

'Mine was a peculiarly happy childhood, a fair field for the sowing of that good seed, the growth of which, alas! has become too frequently impeded by the 'thorns and briars' which have since 'sprung up and choked it.' I was indeed very happy with one dear brother, eighteen months younger than myself, and a father and mother whom no words of mine would be adequate to praise or describe. When an infant of a few months old we went to live in a retired part of Wales, and there my earliest recollections begin, we staid (sic) there eight years.'[2]

[1]Margaret Sandbach, 'To My Brother, On Revisiting An Old House', Giuliano De' Medici-A Drama-With Other Poems, (London: William Pickering, 1842), p.201-202.
[2]Robyn Wyn o Eifion, A short sketch of the life and character of the late Mrs Sandbach, (n.p: n.pub, n.d), .

Here, Margaret forged her deep and long lasting relationship with nature and her love for the Welsh countryside:

Yma, cafodd ei pherthynas ddofn a pharhaol â natur a'i chariad at gefn gwlad Cymru eu meithrin ym Margaret:

'My brother and I, for four or five years were allowed to run wild in the country, to do as we liked out of doors, and to come in and go out as we chose. Three of these years, from five to eight, I remember well - tho' there was, doubtless, more surveillance than we were aware of. My recollections are of perfect freedom, - of wandering in the woods and gardens about the house, - of gathering particular flowers, which we sought in known places from year to year - of making a house of our own, taking assumed names, and keeping this house from day to day, as master and mistress; going to market, and always speaking Welsh, in our own fashion. We were taught very little. At eight years old I could read and write.'[3]

My earliest recollections are of playing in woods carpeted with blue hyacinth when we lived in that land of beauty North Wales and of running wild the whole day long with my only darling brother. We had no 'schooling' then, I never remember learning a lesson; the only tuition I recall is my father teaching me to write, which instead of being trouble to me was a great pleasure. My Mother was fond of painting and taught me to draw – We had no tutor or lesson learning till we were 8 or 9 years old – everything was cheerfulness. Even the one real distress, my passionate temper was dealt with and subdued at last by that dear and excellent father, was robbed of its danger and its pain… Wisely did our parents leave us to learn in our own way how to be happy – to the simple enjoyments of nature and mutual love. Carefully watching the growth and development of moral feeling and leading us by precept and examples to look to a gracious heavenly Father as the giver of all our good – they were content – no forced intellectual progress made prodigies of us – no excitements such as are so plentifully administered to the children of these days fell in our way – no variety of amusing books, no pandering to appetite in the shape of delicacies, no Pantomimes, no Ducrow-ism[4] and yet we were perfectly happy, and had our fill of day long enjoyment, wholesome, simple, natural.[5]

Pystill became a bucolic benchmark. All creative endeavours and pursuits at Hafodunos were an attempt to recreate these formative yet simple pleasures.

Daeth Pistyll yn fesur o fywyd gwledig pur iddi hi. Roedd pob ymgais a diddordeb creadigol oedd ganddi wedi hynny yn Hafodunos yn ymgais i ailgreu'r pleserau cynnar, syml hyn.

[3]Robyn Wyn o Eifion, A short sketch of the life and character of the late Mrs Sandbach, (n.p: n.pub, n.d), .
[4]Andrew Ducrow (1793-1842) was a circus performer and horse trainer, of great fame during the first half of the nineteenth century.
[5]Powys Record Office, MS M/D/SAND/4/4

A beautiful watercolour of Pystill, the Georgian home where Margaret fondly spent her childhood. It was here that her love of the Welsh countryside originated. Flintshire Record Office.

Llun dyfrlliw hyfryd o gartref Sioraidd Margaret, Pistyll, lle treuliodd hi blentyndod hapus. Yma yr enynnwyd ei chariad at gefn gwlad Cymru. Archifdy Sir y Fflint.

To my brother, on revisiting an old house *[Pystill]*

Amid those haunts our happy childhood knew,
Say, did thy heart some early joys renew?
Did memory take thee back to days of yore,
And leave thee for a moment there, once more?

But only for a moment! – thou on me
Didst turn and gaze, and I had looked on thee;
And each beheld in each the altered mien,
No longer thoughtless as it once had been!

And then the tide of memory flowed again
O'er years of deeper joy, and keener pain;
O'er feelings that were slumbering , when we trod,
Hand clasped in infant hand, this verdant sod.

And by that happy power we met again
The forms beloved our eyes shall seek in vain,
Of those who led us through these tangled bowers,
Whose careful hands once trained these wildered flowers.

Sure their dear spirits then looked down and smiled,
And blest with heavenly peace each sorrowing child;
For didst thou not, with all thy sadness, feel
A soothing influence o'er thy spirit steal?

No bitter thoughts, no vain regret we proved,
As we stood silent in the home we loved;
The years that passed within that calm retreat
Wore still for us their aspect mild and sweet.

Let us so live, that future joy be won
For happy memory as time wears on,
To come and bless us like those guileless years,
Undimmed by dark remorse, or sinful fears![6]

[6]Margaret Sandbach, 'To My Brother, On Revisiting An Old House', Giuliano De' Medici – A Drama – With Other Poems, (London: William Pickering, 1842), p. 201-202.

A typical Georgian childhood was plagued by maladies, and even the wealthy Roscoes could not escape in their rural idyll. Here Margaret's mother writes of her concern for William when he was struck by a virulent illness:

'…Willy was…since Friday, really very ill, I hope however I may now say he is beginning to recover, the fever has left… his pulse are [sic] good but he is low and weak beyond anything I ever saw in a child. On Sunday evening he had a blister on the back of his neck to… his head, which he complained much of… He passed an indifferent night, but is certainly better today, he speaks more cheerfully and has taken a little breakfast. Margaret and Edward Henry are very well but I shall think them in luck if they escape the Whooping Cough which just now surrounds us on all sides. I certainly am better since I had my head shaved, the frequent cold application of vinegar and water with which I bath my head many times a day has sustained me more than anything I have tried… I never saw a more patient creature than Will has been, we had scarcely a complaint even during the application of the blister…'[7]

Later, Mrs Roscoe continued to update her mother-in-law on the deteriorating condition:

'…Our brave little sufferer has passed a tolerably composed night and is much the same today - when Dr Cummings left at 9 last night he was inclined to think more favourably of him - his pulses being more regular than in the morning and no imminence of fever which he expected. I had not the least hope of him yesterday and Mr W thought the same - we passed a dreadful day of anxiety you may be sure - indeed it was too much to bear seeing… the effect of the immolars plasters, blisters… Simpson whose conduct is beyond all praise is almost worn out for she has never left night or day. I am as well or better than I can expect…dear Will is certainly no worse, his eyes look hollow - he has egg and wine every hour [and] when very low a little brandy added.'[8]

'…I believe I am feeling the effects of anxiety now Willy is beginning to improve, Ed is gone out to dine, and quite well…'[9]

Roedd afiechydon plentyndod yn gyffredin yn y cyfnod Sioraidd, ac ni lwyddodd hyd yn oed y teulu cefnog Roscoe i'w hosgoi, yno yn eu paradwys wledig. Dyma gofnod mam Margaret yn ei phryder am William wedi iddo ddal afiechyd difrifol:

Adroddodd Mrs Roscoe ragor o'r hanes yn ôl i'w mam-yng-nghyfraith wrth i'r sefyllfa waethygu:

[7]Liverpool, Liverpool Record Office, Roscoe Papers, 920-ROS 3613. From Margaret Roscoe to her mother-in-law, Pystill, June 1815.
[8]Liverpool, Liverpool Record Office, Roscoe Papers, 920-ROS 3614. From Margaret Roscoe to Jane Roscoe, Pystill, June 1815.
[9]Liverpool, Liverpool Record Office, Roscoe Papers, 920-ROS 3615. From Margaret Roscoe whilst at Pystill to Jane Roscoe.

Yn anffodus, dros dro bu'r gwelliant a bu farw William. Cafodd marwolaeth ei brawd hynaf effaith ddofn ar Margaret. Y berthynas agos rhwng brodyr a chwiorydd fu prif destun ei barddoniaeth a'i rhyddiaith wedi hynny.

Sadly the improvement was short-lived and William died. The death of her elder brother had a profound effect upon Margaret. Her poetry and prose would come to be dominated by the relationship between siblings, particularly that of brother and sister.

'I had another brother one year older than myself. He died when five years old. I recollect him, but very indistinctly as to person. I recollect his being taken ill, but do not remember his death; but I remember my mother telling a friend, when I was supposed to be asleep, that they found me that day, after missing me, lying asleep on the bed beside my dead brother. This shows that a child of four years old was not alarmed by the aspect of death on a familiar face. I have thought with pleasure of this - for there must have been a strong infant bond of love between us, to draw me secretly to his side, and lay me down by him in the stillness of his cold sleep.'[10]

Yn ganlyniad i farwolaeth William, ac unigrwydd cymharol Pistyll, closiodd Margaret yn fwyfwy at ei brawd Edward Henry. Roedd hi'n dotio'n llwyr arno ac roeddynt yn gyfeillion mynwesol ar hyd eu hoes. Roedd holl aelodau'r teulu Roscoe yn dioddef o iechyd gwael, a digwyddodd rhywbeth i Edward Henry yn niwedd y 1830au a barodd poen meddwl dybryd iddi hi.

As a result of William's death and the relative isolation of life at Pistyll, Margaret drew closer to her younger brother, Edward Henry, who she doted on and became her closest friend until her own death. All of the Roscoe family suffered from poor health and an incident in the late-1830s affecting Edward Henry caused great anxiety:

[10]Robyn Wyn o Eifion, A short sketch of the life and character of the late Mrs Sandbach, (n.p: n.pub, n.d), . Quoted originally from 'Recollections of My Childhood,' commenced about 1847 but left unpublished.

To my brother in illness

My brother! as I gaze upon thy face
That beamed so late with happy smiles and love,
I weep to see the change! — the love is there
That ever smiled on me, but the bright hope,
The laughing gladness of thy soul is gone!
I look on thee and pray — Oh my beloved!
Thou wilt not leave me! for our God will guard
And watch thy precious life, — to Him I give,
Knowing that he will keep thee, and I place
With faith that bows, yet trembles, all my trust
On that sure Rock of Ages, who afflicts
To bring unto himself the rebel heart!
Upon my knees before the throne of grace,
I supplicate his tender mercy still.
My brother dear! Oh I do love thee so,
That all the world, the sky, the earth, the air,
Look fairer when thou smil'st, that all my hopes
Brighten, when thou art bright, grow dim, when thou
Art clouded by a pain, or grief, or care.

Thou wilt not leave me! Sure thou wilt not go
Before me, to the Spirit Land of light!
My hand-in-hand companion, early friend,
Dear sharer of my sweetest memories!
And yet I could not keep thee —mortal love
Hath not a power to save. Be calm, my heart!
Wait the decree of Him who knows thy prayer,
And answers or denies. He gave thee all,
And if He takes away, still bless His name![11]

Hero grieving over the dead body of Leander by John Gibson. Private Collection.
Hero grieving over the dead body of Leander gan John Gibson. Casgliad Preifat.

[11]Margaret Sandbach, 'To my brother in illness', Poems, (London: William Pickering, 1840), p.89.

Drawing of a bird and flower by Margaret. Private Collection

Llun o aderyn a blodyn gan Margaret. Casgliad Preifat.

Undodiaid oedd y teulu Roscoe, yn credu mai un Duw oedd, yn hytrach na Thrindod y Tad, y Mab a'r Ysbryd Glân.

The Roscoes were a Unitarian family, believing God was a single being rather than the Trinity of Father, Son and Holy Spirit:

'My first idea of God was that of a good, kind and affectionate human being, like my father. Partly from trying to realise a something tangible in my thoughts of God, and partly from a vivid dream I had of being in heaven and seeing Him - this image always rose to my mind's eye, - and even now I can call up distinctly the very attitude and manner of the paternal figure. To my mind, the idea of God as Father was very natural, because to me, my father was everything that was good, and great, and powerful, and protecting. Independent of the sacred tie between us, there was in him much to excite the love and veneration of a child, - of beautiful countenance, tall figure, and frank cheerful manner, which gave an impression of power and strength - he was in heart all that was loving, devoted, and tender, anxious for our highest good, and ever watchful of our outward comfort and happiness. My impressions, therefore, of God were wholly happy. He was my Father in Heaven; and to these earliest impressions are, I doubt not, to be traced the warm religious feelings I afterwards evinced, and the great happiness and comfort I enjoyed in them during a long season of bodily illness.'[12]

The only great sorrow I remember in my early childhood was from having told a lie. I do not recollect telling it, but I recollect well and vividly the remorse that ensued. It was an intolerable burden to me and when the nurse was undressing me at night, I made a confidante of her and confessed my misery. 'When I have done washing you', she said, 'I will take you down to your Papa'. Longing to confess, yet fearing, I was carried down in my nightdress, and when the nurse opened the parlour door, I burst into tears and stretched out my arms to my parents, crying, 'I broke the picture'. My father rose and took me to his breast and folded me there with fond words of forgiveness & encouragement. Oh the sorrow, and the bliss of those moments! I never told a falsehood again.

[12]Robyn Wyn o Eifion, A short sketch of the life and character of the late Mrs Sandbach, (n.p: n.pub, n.d), p.15.

Margaret's mother, Margaret Lace, was a noted writer, publishing Floral Illustrations of the Seasons in 1829. Margaret assisted her with illustrations and research, and it was through her mother that her passion for gardening and the study of flora stemmed.

Roedd Margaret Lace, mam Margaret, yn awdures o fri. Cyhoeddodd Floral Illustrations of the Seasons ym 1829 a bu Margaret yn ei helpu gyda'r darluniau a'r ymchwil. Drwy ei mam y datblygodd Margaret ei brwdfrydedd am arddio ac astudio blodau.

My mother became a real proficient in painting birds after Mr Audubon's[13] manner and about this time she was basically engaged for my Grandfather in making drawings for his work on mountain plants, of which she executed a great portion. She was a great botanist and had a great talent for flower painting – My dear sweet mother! I yearn to see her graceful hand tracing those delicate lines, and her admiring eye dwell on the beauty of those fairest of nature's forms. Flower and a garden have ever been associated with my dearest affections and happiest days.[14]

It was Margaret's mother more than anyone else who encouraged her to write and study natural forms, but also the art of gentility. In 1820, Mrs Roscoe wrote from Pystill that

Mam Margaret yn anad neb oedd yn ei chymell i ysgrifennu ac i astudio ffurfiau natur, a hefyd sut oedd tyfu i fod yn foneddiges. Ym 1820, ysgrifennodd Mrs Roscoe o Pistyll fod

'…Margaret is much pleased with her pin cushion, the little box that contained it was like everything in Edward's bag spoiled with the salt water. I think I shall leave her the folds of this letter to write her thanks, or rather to attempt it, for I don't know that her writing will be very legible. Edward Henry is quite stout, he makes slow progress…and it seems so tiresome to him that I don't urge him too much attention at present…'[15]

A fine watercolour study by Margaret and her mother of a white and crimson chrysanthemum. Published 1829 in Floral Illustrations of the Seasons. Private Collection.

Astudiaeth goeth mewn dyfrlliw gan Margaret a'i mam o flodyn ffarwel haf gwyn a rhuddgoch. Cyhoeddwyd ym 1829 yn Floral Illustrations of the Seasons. Casgliad Preifat.

[13]John James Audubon (1785-1851), a French-American ornithologist and naturalist.
[14]MS M/D/SAND/4/4
[15]Liverpool, Liverpool Record Office, Roscoe Papers, 920-ROS 3615. From Margaret Roscoe to Jane Roscoe, Pystill.

Dyma waith cynnar yr awdures ifanc:

The young writer's first work:

Jane Roscoe (1757-1824), nee Griffies, wife of William Roscoe and Margaret's paternal grandmother. Shown here with her eldest son, William Stanley Roscoe (1782-1843), who went on to become a noted poet, painted by John Williamson. Liverpool Archives.

Jane Roscoe (1757-1824), née Griffies, gwraig William Roscoe a nain Margaret ar ochr ei thad. Peintiwyd hi yma gyda'i mab hynaf, William Stanley Roscoe (1782-1843) gan John Williamson. Archifau Lerpwl.

Opposite: A self portrait by Margaret, dated 1828. Private Collection.

Gyferbyn: Hunanbortread gan Margaret, dyddiedig 1828. Casgliad Preifat.

'Dear Grandmama
I am very much obliged to you for the nice Pincushion you was so good to send me by Papa.
M. Roscoe'[16]

But these days of wild freedom came to an end – we left the beautiful home of our infancy for one in the suburbs of a great town, where we were to lead a new life, but not a less happy one, although so different. Long did the recollection of the scenes we had left dwell on our hearts – the wood walks, the alcove, the pool, the excursions over the hills – how often we talked of these with a sigh, and longed for them again. Even now my mind's eye sees the rich prospect that was spread before our view from that sweet spot, the green meadows in the foreground, the old oak wood (the same where the blue hyacinth grew, and now alas cut down) stretching its rich colouring across the middle distances – behind it the broad estuary of the river Dee and the blue expanse of sea beyond. It was very beautiful and lost nothing now in our estimations by a comparison with brick walls and suburban fields.

O hyn ymlaen, merch â'i chalon yng nghefn gwlad fyddai Margaret a byddai'n dychwelyd i Gymru ar ôl priodi i fyw yn Sir Ddinbych. Yn y cyfamser byddai'n rhaid bodloni ar Lerpwl.

Henceforth, Margaret would always be a country girl at heart and was destined to return to Wales to make her marital home in Denbighshire. But in the intervening years she was to make do with Liverpool.

It was our custom for some years to spend every other Sunday with my Grandfather. We were for a long time the only grandchildren old enough to visit him in this way, but as other members of the family grew older, they took the alternate Sundays. He was surrounded by a happy family, love and harmony prevailed in that circle, and never ever harsh words uttered there. His presence instead of being a restraint upon us was an additional impulse to gaiety and enjoyment. He had always cultivated in his children a habit of cheerful conversation; he never allowed them to bring a book to a meal, and expected the social circle around him to be really sociable. I had an admiration for my Grandfather's appearance which was very venerable, especially his hair, when a child I used to stand by while he curled it with the curling irons, and watch the proceeding with great interest.

[16]Liverpool, Liverpool Record Office, Roscoe Papers, 920-ROS 3617. From Margaret Roscoe to her mother, Pystill, 1820.

A sketch by Margaret of the view to North Wales from the Wirral. Private Collection.

Braslun gan Margaret o'r olygfa i Ogledd Cymru o Gilgwri. Casgliad Preifat.

Taid Margaret ar ochr ei mam, Joshua Lace (1762-1841), oedd sylfaenydd a llywydd cyntaf Cymdeithas y Gyfraith yn Lerpwl. Roedd yn gyfreithiwr ac yn bartner busnes cynnar i William Roscoe, cyn i Roscoe benderfynu nad oedd am barhau â'r gyfraith. Roedd gwraig Joshua, Margaret Lace, née Griffies, yn ferch i Thomas Griffies, adeiladwr o Gaer.

Joshua Lace (1762-1841), Margaret's maternal grandfather, was the founder and first president of the Liverpool Law Society. He was a solicitor and early business partner of William Roscoe, before Roscoe decided that Law was not his preferred profession. Joshua's wife, Margaret Griffies, was the daughter of Thomas Griffies, a builder from Chester.

We had not lost all our country pleasures with the loss of our country home. At Gateacre, the house of our maternal Grandfather Mr Lace, we enjoyed again something of the delightful rural life we had formerly led in Wales - there was a charming old garden with it, orchard, parterres & plantations - its little walks planted with sweet briar, its shady groves of flowering shrubs and there were meadows and hay fields, and the Porch covered with jasmine where we sat and listened to the birds singing in the old pear tree, from which we used to shake down the ripe sugary pears. There was no wandering over wild hills, or down deep oak woods – no free and careless life of play; but the calm and gentle routine of country pleasures, subject to mild rules and wholesome laws…

Our [Lace] Grandparents deserved a warm place in our hearts – both totally different in character but uniformly kind and affectionate to us. She, the gentlest of human beings, he, one of the most just and most stern of men. He was a person of strongly marked character, of unbending integrity, keen observation and clear judgement, a reverent love of truth and great industry and perseverance. There was about him with all this a love of fun and drollery which made him an amusing companion even to children, but we stood in awe of him and feared greatly to offend him.

These days passed in the country I look back upon with gratitude and affection; besides that they were in themselves very happy, they helped keep alive in our hearts that early love of nature which had formed such large a portion of the happiness of the past, and cultivated for us yet to the taste for simple pleasures independent of such worldly circumstances which I look upon as one of the main sources of happiness in life, and to which I attribute much of that ecstatic cheerfulness which has been a blessing to us through succeeding years.

Margaret's formative years had been spent in the Welsh countryside, learning to closely observe nature. The small and close-knit family had suffered tragedy but she was equipped with fortitude and faith, which would stand her in good stead for adult life. Unknowingly, Margaret followed Gibson's footsteps to the circle of her grandfather in Liverpool; the city where her future husband awaited.

Treuliodd Margaret ei blynyddoedd cynnar yng nghefn gwlad Cymru, gan ddysgu sut i wylio natur. Roedd y teulu bychan clòs wedi dioddef sawl trychineb ond roedd ganddi hi'r nerth a'r ffydd fyddai yn ei chynnal drwy ei hoes. Heb yn wybod iddi hi, dilynnodd Margaret yn ôl troed Gibson ac ymuno â chymdeithas ei thaid yn Lerpwl lle byddai'n cyfarfod â'r dyn fyddai'n ŵr iddi hi.

This terracotta medallion of William Roscoe by John Gibson is dated 1813. According to the British Museum, the medallion 'is an important example of Gibson's work before he went to Rome. It was seen by contemporaries as one of the best portraits of Roscoe.' British Museum

Mae'r dyddiad 1813 ar y medaliwn terracotta hwn o William Roscoe gan John Gibson. Yn ôl yr Amgueddfa Brydeinig, mae'n enghraifft bwysig o waith Gibson cyn iddo fynd i Rufain. Credai ei gyfoedion bod hwn yn un o'r portreadau gorau o Roscoe. Yr Amgueddfa Brydeinig.

A watercolour of the coast at Abergele by Margaret. Private Collection.

Llun dyfrlliw o'r arfordir ger Abergele gan Margaret. Casgliad Preifat.

II

'I do so like your lines, dear Emmes, I think them beautiful, and you ought really to let people see your verses, and not bury your talents in a napkin'[1]

A dashing portrait miniature of Henry Robertson Sandbach (1807-1895), aged around 26, portraying him around the time of his marriage to Margaret in 1833. Private Collection.

Portread miniatur bywiog o Henry Robertson Sandbach (1807-1895) pan oedd rhyw 26 mlwydd oed a thua'r adeg y priododd â Margaret yn 1833. Casgliad Preifat.

Wyddom ni ddim sut y bu i Henry a Margaret gyfarfod, efallai yn Lerpwl, efallai yn un o'r dawnsfeydd ffurfiol oedd yn y ddinas honno bryd hynny. Ymddengys mai cariad pur a barodd i'r ddau ddyweddïo.

We do not know how Henry and Margaret met, but it was in Liverpool, perhaps at one of the great balls that were frequently held in the city during the period. Their engagement was a love-match:

Liverpool
6th May 1831

My dear Mary

Look very serious - I am going to give you a piece of news that will astonish you - but I hope please you too. I am going to be married to --- Miss Margaret Roscoe.

I do not know when - for our Papas & Mamas think we ought to wait 12 months. When you come here you shall know her and when you know her you shall tell me how you like her. I understand you are so much changed that I shall have to make your acquaintance anew - so that she & I can learn to know you together…

Believe me Dear Mary
your affectionate Brother, Henry R Sandbach[2]

Nid gwraig yn unig oedd Margaret i Henry; hi oedd ei ysbrydoliaeth. Cafodd ei chefndir rhyddfrydig effaith barhaol ar ei gŵr. Drwy gelfyddyd, llenyddiaeth a hanes, llwyddodd ei dylanwad addfwyn feithrin nawdd o bwysigrwydd cenedlaethol yn Henry, a oedd i barhau ynddo wedi ei marwolaeth hi. Cartref Henry a Margaret oedd tŷ fferm to gwellt o'r enw The Cottage ar dir y Woodlands, cartref y teulu Sandbach yn Aigburth, Lerpwl.

For Henry, Margaret represented not only a wife but a reforming light, and her liberal background became entrenched in Henry's own outlook. Her gentle influence through art, literature and history, cultivated a patronage of national importance in him that was to outlive her. Henry and Margaret lived in a large thatched farmhouse, called The Cottage, in the grounds of the Sandbach family home Woodlands at Aigburth, Liverpool.

[1]Centre for Buckinghamshire Studies, D115/11/48
[2]Powys Record Office, M/D/SAND/5/1267. Henry R Sandbach to Mary Williams, stating his intention to marry Margaret Roscoe
[3]Margaret Sandbach, 'A Dream', Aurora and other poems, (London: Pickering, 1850), p.122-3.

A Dream

I DREAMT thou didst not love me. Oh, what anguish
Wrung my sad heart, as on thy face I gazed!
Heard the cold tone, saw the cold eyes averted,
To which in fond beseeching, mine were raised.
I dreamt that thou , with altered voice, reproached me,
And sharply fell thy words upon mine ear;
And in my breast arose the bitter feeling,
The blighting knowledge, that I was not dear.
It seemed as though that moment, all the fountains
Of joy within my soul, to ice were turned;
And chilly silence, and despairing sorrow,
Entered where love had once so brightly burned.
It was as if upon the blushing Spring-time,
The freezing winter laid his death-cold hand,
And hushed the melodies, and checked the beauty,
And bound young Nature in his iron band.

In silent anguish, o'er my poisoned slumber,
I felt the pressure of the cruel dream;
And woke to question why 'twas sent to grieve me, —
Oh why, beloved one, why thus altered seem?
Is it because thy spirit far above me,
Is all too pure to mingle with mine own,
That bound to earth too strongly, does not seek thee
In the clear heaven of holiness alone?
But do not thou forsake me! Lead me upward,
Nearer to thee, and nearer to our God:
Ah, if the light of thy dear love desert me,
Cheerless I faint upon my earthly road.[3]

Miniature painting of Margaret Sandbach (1812-1852)
from the time of her marriage by an unknown artist. Private Collection.

Paentiad miniatur o Margaret Sandbach (1812-1852)
gan artist anhysbys tua chyfnod ei phriodas. Casgliad Preifat.

Henry was frequently away, working for his father's business or overseeing improvements at Hafodunos.

Henry's letters to Margaret during the early years of their marriage were often comforting his young wife, who, aged only twenty, was in charge of her own household and found life away from her parents and brother rather lonely.

Roedd Henry oddi cartref yn aml, yn gweithio ym musnes ei dad, neu'n cadw golwg ar y gwelliannau yn Hafodunos.

Mae llythyrau Henry at Margaret yn ystod blynyddoedd cynnar eu bywyd priodasol yn aml yn cysuro ei wraig ifanc. A hithau ond yn ugain mlwydd oed, hi oedd yn gyfrifol am redeg ei chartref ac yn aml yn teimlo'n unig gan weld eisiau ei rhieni a'i brawd.

Hester Sandbach (1813-1837) was the first wife of William Robertson Sandbach and they were married on May 9th 1837; she sadly died on October 27th later that year, in Paris. Margaret was a witness at their wedding. Henry wrote to Margaret a few days after Hester's death: 'the doctors seem to think she injured herself by taking so much blue pill - which was unsuitable for her situation - her complaint was inflammation of the whole intestinal canal - from the mouth to the throat, stomach, intestine, etc - due to her constant habit of taking sundiam.' Private Collection.

Hester Sandbach (1813-1837), oedd gwraig gyntaf William Robertson Sandbach, a briododd ar 9 Mai 1837, ond yn anffodus bu hi farw ym Mharis ar 25 Hydref y flwyddyn honno. Roedd Margaret yn dyst yn eu priodas. Ysgrifennodd Henry at Margaret rai dyddiau wedi marwolaeth Hester: 'the doctors seem to think she injured herself by taking so much blue pill - which was unsuitable for her situation - her complaint was inflammation of the whole intestinal canal - from the mouth to the throat, stomach, intestine etc - due to her constant habit of taking sundiam.' Casgliad Preifat.

6th November 1836
Hafodunos

My dear wife,

It is Sunday morning and while my father & Mr Horsfall are gone to hear the Welsh service at the church. --- it grieved me to find you were so poorly and in such low spirits. Do not give way to the feelings you express, for while nothing makes me so happy as to see you happy, nothing grieves me more than to see you sad and sorrowful except to be myself the cause of that sorrow. I am unconscious that I have said anything to wound your feelings, if I have, it was most unintentional, and therefore my dear girl forgive and forget it - in your own words -

'do not doubt that all is well
for still around thee beams his love
and keep their eye with steadfast gaze
still fixed upon the star above'

- your book of Poetry is a great delight to me. I read it every night, before I pray for you, and go to rest. What sad thought is always haunting you? I do not know at all but there is a never failing source of comfort in prayer…I like Hafodunos better every time I come - My dear girl I know you have devoted yourself to my happiness, have I not loved you for it, and fed upon your love. Let us be more one than ever. I do not mean alone, but when not alone in every situation - let us understand each other and act with one impulse united by the subtle sympathies of fond confiding affections…will you write a hymn today, your hymns are beautiful, and a love song by the time I get home –

Your affectionate and devoted husband…[4]

Pan fu farw ei thad ym 1834, daeth Edward Henry, ei hunig frawd oedd wedi goroesi, yn benteulu. Cafodd y llysenw 'Emmes', a bu Margaret yn llythyru'n gyson ag ef drwy gydol ei bywyd.

Margaret's surviving brother, Edward Henry, became head of the family on the death of their father in 1834. Known by his pet name, 'Emmes', Margaret maintained regular correspondence with Edward Henry throughout her life.

[4]Powys Record Office, M/D/SAND/8/6

Their widowed mother, Margaret Roscoe, affectionately referred to as 'Mrs', continued to be a dominant force in their lives.

Aigburth
May 8th 1837

My Dearest Emmes,

I wrote to you lately (by Issaverdens, who went on Saturday) that I have but little to tell you as to news or incident of any sort. The wedding to take place tomorrow, is the principal event going, at present among us…I have heard today that a party of Henry's friends from Holland are coming to stay with us, Mr and Mrs Vander Undermenlen, and Miss Dedel, (I am afraid I shall call her Ladle) their sister. They are now in London. The Lady can speak no English (alas for my poor tongue, what will it do with French?) …What pleasures it would have given our dear father to have heard of our success - it would have been some reward for his anxiety and his toils - our bright spot in his life of sorrow - for so it was in many respects ever since his marriage. The greatest consolation to us is to think he had comfort in his home. I often wished I had never left him! - Harry sends his best love to you. Goodbye dearest, I don't know when you'll have this. Yours Ever MS.[5]

Henry and Margaret made a Continental tour in 1838 and 1839 through the Netherlands, Germany and Switzerland into Italy; visiting Hamburg, Frankfort, Geneva, Genoa, Rome, and Naples; returned again through France. It was during this grand tour that Margaret met John Gibson; a meeting that would change both their lives forever.

Parhaodd ei mam, Margaret Roscoe, oedd bellach yn weddw, i gael dylanwad cryf ar eu bywydau. Cyfeiriwyd ati'n annwyl fel 'Mrs'.

Ym 1838 a 1839 aeth Henry a Margaret ar daith i'r Cyfandir. Aethant drwy'r Iseldiroedd, yr Almaen a'r Swistir i'r Eidal, gan ymweld â Hamburg, Frankfurt, Genefa, Genova, Rhufain a Napoli cyn dychwelyd drwy Ffrainc. Yn ystod y Daith Fawr hon cyfarfu Margaret â John Gibson, cyfarfyddiad fyddai'n newid bywyd y ddau am byth.

William Robertson Sandbach (1813-1892), Henry's younger brother, who firstly married Hester Willink (1813-1837), and later married Sara M Van Capellan (1807 - 1881). This portrait, based on the preliminary sketch, can be dated to 1837. Private Collection.

William Robertson Sandbach (1813-1892). Brawd iau Henry, a briododd Hester Willink (1813-1837) yn gyntaf ac yna Sara M Van Capellan (1807-1881). Seiliwyd y portread hwn ar fraslun cynharach a luniwyd ym 1837. Casgliad Preifat.

[5]Centre for Buckinghamshire Studies D115/N/66, Margaret to Edward Henry Roscoe, Aigburth, May 8th 1837.

'John Gibson RA, from a miniature painted by Thomas Griffiths and finished the morning that Mr Gibson left Liverpool for Rome.' Private Collection. Casgliad Preifat.

Er y byddai perthynas Margaret a Gibson yn un grymus, roedd ef yn bedwar deg wyth cyn iddynt gyfarfod. Dau ddeg chwech oedd Margaret. Pan ddechreuodd Margaret a Henry chwilio am gysylltiadau ei theulu hi yn Rhufain, roedd Gibson eisoes yn enwog fel cerflunydd rhyngwladol. Roedd hi'n daith bell i gyfarfod bachgen o Gyffin yng Ngogledd Cymru.

Ganwyd John Gibson yn fab i arddwr masnachol mewn pentref ger muriau Castell Conwy. Ŵyr neb fawr am ei fywyd cynnar. Pan oedd yn un ar bymtheg, safai gyda'i deulu ar ymyl y doc yn Lerpwl yn barod i ymfudo i America. Ond cafodd ei fam ormod o fraw wrth feddwl am groesi'r Iwerydd yn y llong oedd o'i blaen. Daeth Lerpwl yn gartref dros dro iddo.

Gallai Gibson yn hawdd fod wedi methu ar ei alwedigaeth. Cafodd gynnig bod yn brentis i beintiwr portreadau, ond allai'i dad ddim talu'r costau. Cafodd waith gyda saer dodrefn, lle dysgodd gerfio coed ac addurno dodrefn. Yna cafodd brentisiaeth gyda saer maen i wneud cerrig beddau, silffoedd pen tân a'u tebyg. Yma y cyfarfu Gibson â William Roscoe, taid Margaret, oedd yn ŵr pwysig a dysgedig, ac a welodd dalent yn y gŵr ifanc a rhoddodd rwydd hynt iddo ddefnyddio'i lyfrgell sylweddol. Yma astudiodd Gibson y ffurfiau clasurol a ddaeth yn ysbrydoliaeth iddo yn ei waith.

Datblygodd ei ddawn ac yn saith ar hugain mlwydd oed roedd yn gerflunydd heb ei ail yn Lerpwl. Cafodd gynnig gwaith yn Llundain a Rhufain. Dewisodd Rufain a theithiodd i'r Ddinas Dragwyddol. Bu'n gweithio yn stiwdio y cerflunydd enwog, Antonio Canova (1757-1822) gan greu gweithiau yn y dull 'Delfrydol', yn ogystal â phenddelwau 'ffansi' dychmygol a cherfluniau darluniadol.

Although Margaret and Gibson were to form such an intense relationship, they didn't meet until he was forty-eight years old. Margaret was already twenty-six. When Margaret and Henry looked up her family connections on arriving in Rome, Gibson had established himself as a sculptor with an international reputation; it was a long way to go to meet a boy from Gyffin in North Wales.

John Gibson was born the son of a market gardener in the village adjacent to the walls of Conwy Castle. Little is known of his early years. When he was sixteen, his family were standing on the dock in Liverpool, ready to emigrate to America. But when his mother took fright at the thought of crossing the Atlantic in the ship before them, Liverpool was to become his home, for a while at least.

Gibson could quite easily have missed out on finding his vocation. An apprenticeship to a portrait artist was offered, only for the fees to be out of reach of his father's pocket. He was then taken on by a cabinet maker, where he learned to carve wood and ornament furniture. Eventually, he was apprenticed to a marble mason; making funerary work, fireplaces and the like. It was here that Gibson met Margaret's grandfather William Roscoe; a powerful and educated gentleman who spotted the young man's talent and gave him access to his impressive library. Here, the young Gibson studied the classical forms that were to become his stock in trade.

His work progressed and at twenty seven, Gibson was the preeminent sculptor in Liverpool. Receiving offers to work in London and Rome, he opted for the latter and made for the eternal city. Working at the studio of the famous sculptor Antonio Canova (1757-1822), Gibson produced work in the 'Ideal' style, including both 'fancy' busts from the imagination and portrait statues.

The following year he opened his own studio, produced his first full-size figure (a sleeping shepherd boy) and was introduced to the Duke of Devonshire, an influential collector. In 1819, he began a large scale work, which was to become his Mars and Cupid. On seeing this work, the Duke ordered a copy; this was his first major commission and was to launch his reputation to a new level. Mars and Cupid arrived at the Duke's home, Chatsworth, six years later and was much admired. When Canova passed away in 1822, the Danish sculptor Bertel Thorvaldsen (1770-1844) took Canova's mantle and filled the role of Gibson's mentor in Rome.

Throughout his forties, Gibson was riding high. Honoured by the Academy of St. Luke in Rome, and then made a Royal Academician by the august London Institution, Gibson kept up his Welsh connections, taking Mary Lloyd (1819 – 1896) of Hengwrt into his studio and becoming friends with the Merthyr-born artist Penry Williams (c.1800 – 1885). Gibson was by now a leading figure of the British artistic colony in Rome. His busy studio employed many workmen and assistants, carvers and students. His brother Ben (1811 - 1851) joined him and worked as a carver, copying his many works and contributing his knowledge of classical literature and antiquities. Amidst the pointing, ornament cutting and marble polishing he welcomed many grand and titled visitors, such as the Duke of Bavaria and a Grand Duke (later to be Tsar Alexander II) of Russia.

It was into this milieu that Margaret stepped with Henry, curious to meet her countryman, the great sculptor who had been set on his course by her own grandfather.

Y flwyddyn ganlynol, agorodd ei stiwdio'i hun a lluniodd ei gerflun cyntaf o faintioli llawn (bugail ifanc yn cysgu). Cafodd ei gyflwyno i Ddug Dyfnaint oedd yn gasglwr o fri ac ym 1819 dechreuodd ar waith mawr a ddatblygodd yn ddelwedd o'r duwiau Mawrth a Ciwpid. Wedi gweld y gwaith, archebodd y Dug gopi ohono. Dyma'i gomisiwn cyntaf a chynyddodd enwogrwydd Gibson. Cyrhaeddodd Mars and Cupid gartref y Dug yn Chatsworth chwe blynedd yn ddiweddarach a chafodd ei edmygu'n fawr. Pan fu farw Canova ym 1822, y cerflunydd o Ddenmarc, Bertel Torvaldsen (1770-1844) a ysgwyddodd ei gyfrifoldebau ac ef fu mentor Gibson yn Rhufain.

Tra yn ei bedwardegau roedd Gibson ar flaen y gad. Derbyniodd anrhydedd gan Academi Sant Luc yn Rhufain a daeth yn aelod o'r Academi Frenhinol yn Llundain. Cadwodd Gibson ei gysylltiadau Cymreig gan wahodd Mary Lloyd (1819-1896) o Hengwrt i'w stiwdio a dod yn gyfaill i Penry Williams (c.1800-1885) oedd yn hanu o Ferthyr Tudful. Erbyn hyn, Gibson oedd y mwyaf blaenllaw ym mysg yr artistiaid Prydeinig yn Rhufain. Rhoddodd waith i lawer yn ei stiwdio brysur, yn gerfwyr ac yn fyfyrwyr. Daeth ei frawd Ben (1811-1851) ato a gweithiodd fel cerfiwr gan gopïo darnau o'i waith a chyfrannu o'i wybodaeth am lenyddiaeth glasurol a henebion. Yn ogystal â gwaith pwyntio, creu addurniadau a chaboli'r marmor ef hefyd oedd yn croesawu llawer o'r ymwelwyr nodedig megis Dug Bafaria ac Archddug Rwsia (a ddaeth wedi hynny yn Tsar Alexander II).

I ganol y gymdeithas hon y daeth Margaret a Henry, hithau'n awyddus i gyfarfod â'i chydwladwr, y cerflunydd enwog a roddwyd ar ben ei ffordd gan ei thaid.

Margaret's drawing of a windmill on the coast of Belgium. Private Collection.
Lluniad Margaret o felin wynt ar arfordir Gwlad Belg. Casgliad Preifat.

A scene drawn by Margaret during her grand tour of Italy. Private Collection.

Golygfa a ddarluniwyd gan Margaret yn ystod ei Thaith Fawr yn yr Eidal. Casgliad Preifat.

2nd July 1838

Dear Emmes,

…If it is as beautiful a day in England as in Belgium, the Coronation will indeed be brilliant. I am thinking so of you and wondering where you are. We are detained here, (a la 'Pully Bridge') for want of horses. Oh I have longed for you to see the creatures called post horses here you would laugh, till you could laugh no more and our great cart horses, lumbering along, with a bit of old patched harness, and ropes for reins, and … a saddle as high as a pillow, and a man in scarlet and gold sitting there on, with a pair of boots nearly up to his hips, and a long whip, which he cracks in a manner enough to distract one - but all description cannot give you an idea of the reality.

…Brussels is a beautiful town; the house so white and clean looking and such fine architecture looked quite brilliant against the blue sky, when I looked out the first morning, our hotel was in the 'Place Royale' where there were 3 other hotels. It is a very large square with the statue of Liberty in the middle, and the Church of St. Jacques at the top. Every evening the soldiers came into the square and beat the retreat, with military towns, but I like the music very much…

…You can't think dearest Emmes how desolate and melancholy I felt at first in a strange land, I am getting over that feeling now - it was being away so far from those I love most of all on Earth and oh how glad I shall be to see your dear face again my own Emm! I have been suffering from the heat the last day or two but today I am quite well, it is very cool and refreshing. I feel weak yet but expect to gain strength every day. Henry is very careful of me and always watching and doing things for me…[6]

Baden
Thursday July 19th 1838

Dearest Emmes,

…After I wrote to you on Saturday, I was taken poorly, as Henry has been in the morning, with sickness and disturbance in my intestine - he got better by night, but I was really quite ill, and by the first attack had gone off. I had such pain in my limbs and feverishness that early next morning H fetched Dr Hutton who prescribed some, draughts which soon cured me with the aid of bed all Sunday… Henry was very queer for a day or two and we have only just got over it! It was a very strange thing and I cannot conceive what it was, nor can I account for the attack -for I had avoided fruit, whereas Henry… had feasted on cherries - but it could not be that, as I was the same – however, we were not very bad, as one professional visit sufficed from the Dr. though he called afterwards in a friendly way.

[6]Centre for Buckinghamshire Studies, D115/10/67, Margaret to Edward Henry Roscoe, 2nd July 1838.
[7]Centre for Buckinghamshire Studies, D115/10/63. Margaret to Edward Henry Roscoe, Baden, 19th July 1838.
[8]Margaret Sandbach, 'Song from the Italian', Poems, (London: William Pickering, 1840), p.111.

…I am or rather have been since I came here rather weak with a 'little Cholesta', and I think it is the air of the place for Henry is affected also - but well enough - I hope it would not affect your 'tummy'… They say I look a great deal brighter and better the last week or two…[7]

Verona
Tuesday Evening 16th October 1838

Dearest Emmes,

…Pray write to me soon my my dearest Emmes, and tell me particularly what you think of Mrs' health, without reserve, and what Uncle Reginald thinks about that little lump. Which I trust may prove to be only a glandular swelling and indeed I felt little alarm about it when I left home particularly after speaking to Uncle Rd about it, for he did seem to think much of it but certainly it is a very anxious thing when there is the slightest threatening of anything serious and it must… make me, and you too, uneasy, until as I hope, any tendency to increase, may disappear. The knowledge of what poor Aunt Martha suffered makes one more anxious and the idea of our dearest mother having anything of the kind in prospect is agonising to think of, but I trust in God, and pray that it may not be so! It was very odd that before I left Geneva I got very uneasy about it, fancying it got worse. And it is much better dear Emmes that I should know exactly how it is, and what Archer thinks, and Uncle Rd because if I don't, I shall always be imagining it worse than it is - to be sure and tell me all you know - you may be sure that you are doing me a real kind help. I will add our address, beyond Florence, before I close this… The little Tavern, dirty hole, full of rough men and soldiers. We tried to sleep in the carriage as night came on. I could not, for sheer weariness - got out, found there was an old straw bed in a kind of loft, lay down half undressed, as snug as could be and slept. Henry lay down in his clothes. Miss Williams went inside the carriage, guarded by Mr. Thomas on the dickey. We got to Milan between one and 2, very glad to rest at last, established ourselves in the Albergo Reale - an Inn said to be the best, and very respectably kept - but oh so dull! …The Duomo, La Scala, and the gate called the Triumphant Arch, now the 'Arch of Peace', 'Auo della Pace' a most beautiful work, also in marble, crowned by a car of victory drawn by 6 colossal horses in bronze, are the things best worth seeing in Milan, and when you add a few pictures in the Breza, and in the …Library - that is all. As to the town I did not like it - hardly any handsome streets; even the Corso is no great thing…

Isola dei Pescatori by Margaret. Private Collection.
Isola dei Pescatori gan Margaret. Casgliad Preifat.

Song from the Italian

Oh tell me why, when far from thee
My spirit is not glad,
And sighs that rend my weeping heart
Compel me to be sad?

And tell me why, when near to thee
My heaving breast is stilled,
And with a pure celestial joy,
My trembling soul is filled?

Why, when my eyes are closed in sleep
Does one like thee appear,
And seems to stand before me then
Thine image, ever dear?

Why does no other beauty seem
So beautiful to me,
Ah tell me why my every thought
Is given alone to thee?[8]

The Road to the Waterfall Beyond Geroldsau, Margaret's sketch of the road to the Geroldsau Waterfall near to Baden, in the Black Forest, Germany. Private Collection.

The Road to the Waterfall Beyond Geroldsau, braslun gan Margaret o'r ffordd at Raeadr Geroldsau ger Baden yn y Schwarzwald, yr Almaen. Casgliad Preifat.

...Venice is not as far from Milan as London from Liverpool and yet we shan't get there till the 4th day! We stopped in passing to see Verona, where we slept. It is a very curious old place. The house of the Capulets is still there and the arms of Juliet's father over the door. ...The Vineyards are very picturesque now, some grapes are not yet gathered, but we meet peasants constantly laden with them, and also cartloads of the crushed fruit, ready to make wine. We get as many bunches as we can eat whenever we like, and find them very refreshing and when we stop to change horses women bring baskets of fruit figs, grapes, pomegranites, pears etc etc all very prettily grouped, with vine leaves to the carriage windows. ...You would be amused at the Scarlet runners. They are not so numerous here as in Switzerland, where they are in troops - one boy as we came from Chansons Et in the car would not go though we had given ... our small money and it told him 'he had no more' upon which the lad replied 'perhaps the Postillion can lend you some' their impudence exceeds everything - but some of them were fine fellows. Sometimes when they come begging round Mr Thomas, he jumps at them with a kind of yell at which they laugh and run off. He is the queerest old man I ever saw, but very good tempered and ready, and a most comfortable servant in every way. I laugh - he says the names of the places where we've been, he calls Namus, Manuse, a promenade, a paramade ect but I am taking up my paper with nonsense. Yet I can't help thinking of my dear Emmes when anything funny comes in my way and there H and J say how you would be amused - but I have not many amusing incidents in 'general'. I have taken a few sketches here and there since I have been better and one of my favourite occupations now is writing , or trying to write a little poem, which is addressed to you dearest Emmes and about Italy etc. I am attempting it in Spenserian Stanza, which is rather difficult... Poetic land as it is, in some respects, there is enough to put all poetry out of one's head, when one comes in cold, into a colder room, and the queer ways of the people!...[9]

Rome
22nd December 1838

My dearest Emmes,

You will be amused at the fine picture in this paper; I cannot resist sending you a letter on it to give you a kind of idea where we are staying. The hotel is the large building on the right, and our windows are the first floor on the left, just above that carriage – so you may fancy that old Emmes looking out of that window where I've put a little dot, is where I often sit – one of our windows also houses the corner and looks in to the drive Monte Pincio, which you enter by that iron gate at the corner of the hotel. It really is very like the place, so please excuse the coarseness of the paper, which certainly is not very ladylike – the obelisk is Egyptian and is in the centre of the Picasso, (the Picasso del Popolo) which you have often heard described as by far the finest part of modern Rome...

[9]Centre for Buckinghamshire Studies, D115/10/59. Margaret to Edward Henry Roscoe, Verona, 16th October 1838.

There are two other magnificent fountains, one which you see in the semicircle under Monte Pincio, and the other is in the opposite semi-circle and statues in white marble all along the sides. Monte Pincio is laid out in terraces as you see – and from the top there is a very fine view of Rome.

…Rome is full of everything, of English, and other strangers but chiefly the former. I must now, dearest Emmes, thank you for your kind welcome letter which I received here. I was delighted to get it and shall be so glad whenever you will send another. Though you say you have not much news to tell, your letters always seem to me full of interesting matter (as Granny says). I fear, dear Emmes, your interior is not strong yet as you say the cold affects you. Do you wear a flannel belt? I say it must be a great safeguard. I know you will be glad to hear I am much better - indeed I have not felt so well for many a long day as I have done all of this week. I can take a long breath and feel no impediments, and my cough is better. You cannot think what a relief this is to me. For ever since my cold at Venice and often before then I had suffered great pain in my chest and sometimes in my side and at one time thought of consulting a Doctor.

However, as my general health kept pretty well I thought best to wait till I got here and now I am a different creature - for the first week I did not feel any better and thought Italy would be a failure after all. - Until the last week I had almost despaired of gaining any good, and now I am in excellent hopes dear Emmes of appearing before you as fat and healthy as if I had never been ill - then how casually I hope that you may be well and jolly too, and then we will have such fun when I come to London, and we'll try the new carriage and go to Richmond in it and what won't we do!! My heart jumps when I think of landing at Dover.

…Henry is quite delighted with Rome and do you know he speaks Italian already - he is certainly sharp at languages. Our Master Signor Ropi (a friend) of Mr Earles says he has a very correct pronunciation - as to me I am a perfect dummy at speaking - H has gone this morning to the top of St. Peters - it is the most splendid building imagination can conceive - and the interior is so beautifully finished and decorated with marbles, mosaics and sculpture - but the streets of Rome!! The filthiest horrible places!! As towns, the Italian cities are miserable, I think except in a few parts that are striking - the fountains for instance are noble large reservoirs of clear water throwing up jets against the sky and giving a picturesque effect we don't see in England. But give me London for a town! A back street there is worth one of the best here. But then, ancient Rome is something quite unique. I have been very much struck with what I have seen of it. But that is not much yet. I shall tell you more in my next…[10]

Illustration of Rome, an intricate illustration engraved as the letterhead on one of Margaret's letters to Edward Henry, showing the rooms which they rented in Rome, marked by the letter X. Private Collection.

Illustration of Rome, darluniad cywrain a ysgythrwyd fel pennawd i un o lythyrau Margaret at Edward Henry, yn nodi'r ystafelloedd oedd ganddynt dan rent yn Rhufain gyda'r llythyren X. Casgliad Preifat.

[10]Centre for Buckinghamshire Studies, D115/10/58. Margaret to Edward Henry Roscoe, Rome, 22nd December 1838.

A study of Margaret's head by John Gibson, chalk on paper, dated March 20th 1839, Rome. Private Collection.

Astudiaeth o ben Margaret gan John Gibson, sialc ar bapur, dyddiedig 20 Mawrth 1839, Rhufain. Casgliad Preifat.

Rome
Monday 7th January 1839

…I am very anxious to write to you, for I have been very uneasy since I heard Mrs had been, after all, obliged to see the London Drs. I think it is much better they should have this advice, and I am very much relieved that the examination has been thoroughly undertaken and the tumour found to be decidedly not what was feared - but still dearest Emmes, I fear her health is a good deal broken lately and I cannot tell you how anxious I am about her. She certainly closes her last letter (the one from London) in more cheerful spirits, but I can see that she was but poorly… I am so afraid of being at all misleaded by letters, and thinking her better than she is, when she is really poorly, and requiring my care and attendance.

Night and day I am thinking of this, and the blisters will make her neck too sore, and I fear will make her very weak. Oh dear Emmes, nobody knows what I feel when I think I have come away for my own sake, and that both duty and inclination demands that I should be with her, to take care of her when she is poorly! You know I did it all for the best, and little thought she would be suffering and anxious as she has been, during my absence, or I would never have left! Would you please dear Emmes, if I am not giving you too much trouble… write to me after receiving this - it would be such a comfort to me, I fear she had a painful examination with Brody but the result seems to have cheered her - I hope to hear by next post how she bore the journey home - what a comfort it is that she has got such a good kind maid!

…I have really enjoyed the last few weeks very much among the wonderful attractions of this place. It is a kind of fascination that dwells in the studios' and etc. here, as far as statuary goes, I suppose there is no place like Rome, and the art is now reaching such a perfection that as Byron says, 'we turn away, dazzled and drunk with beauty' - I shall have such a deal to tell you when I come home, my dearest Emmes, and it won't be too [sic] long now, for we shall soon be setting off. Henry is very kind and sympathizing in my anxieties and does all he can to make me less anxious, but I think he is rather anxious himself - about Mrs - we have certainly had a great deal of pleasure in Italy, and are quite satisfied with our visit - we have often longed for you to share with us - I shall be sorry to leave our kind Gibson, who is our most intimate acquaintance here, and is a delightful man - did you know, dear Emmes, that he is teaching me to model?

He is a very great man, much trusted by the great people, and dines very often with the Duke of Devonshire, Sutherland etc. but he is the simplest, most retiring creature in the world - while he is full of genius - Yesterday we saw a ceremony in one of the Churches here of a .. Lady taking the Veil. It was very interesting but we could not see all we wished, as she did not take the vows, nor was her hair cut off, as she only entered the Convent as a novice - She was splendidly dressed and jewels and diamonds sparkled in her beautiful fair hair. It was not dark like an Italiano - She is a Countess… and very rich - and only 20 years old - only think of her going into that dull hole among nuns! Her gown was embroidered with gold, and her hair of rich satin also embroidered - her de[missing] was white and a white veil hung neatly to her feet.

Botanical studies found in Margaret's sketchbook from the Grand Tour. Private Collection.

Enghreifftiau botanegol o lyfr braslunio Margaret wedi'i Thaith Fawr. Casgliad Preifat.

After [missing] crowned at the Altar by a fine old Cardinal, as the 'Bride of Christ' - she was unrobed … at the back of the altar, and dressed by the Lady ..in a nun's dress - the old Lady then kissed her, and then the triumphant music burst forth in full chorus humouring her praises and his happiness in giving up the …! The music was beautiful and the decorations of the church very splendid… A great many English were there. The Duchess of Sutherland, the Burkingstons etc… we are going, the same party, to see the statues in the Vatican on Friday evening by candle light! They say it is very grand, but I can't enjoy anything now; I feel so anxious about dear Mrs, and thinking of her sore blister! …I take great care of myself, but in spite of all I have got a cold in in my head that smothers me - but does not touch my chest - no cold has, since Venice which shows chest is stronger… we live as quiet as mice and it is this that helps to keep me well…[11]

Detail of Henry Sandbach bust. Photographed by Antonia Dewhurst. Private Collection.

Golwg agos o benddelw Henry Sandbach. Ffotograff gan Antonia Dewhurst. Casgliad Preifat.

Rome
Friday 8th February 1839

Dearest Emmes,

…I have still to thank you for your long delightful letter, which I received a day or two ago after sending of my last to you….It was a very cold day, the day I got it, a piercing North wind, and on my way home from Gibsons, only a few steps I felt the bad pain in my chest which I had not felt for a long time. I ran in a horrid fright and rubbed it with some sharp liniment, then sat down and read your letter, which drove my fright and all away, and thank goodness that once is the only time I have really felt my chest for the last 2 months or more, and I keep very well…But I have a great deal to tell you and must not waste my paper in ecstasies. In the first place perhaps you have heard from Mrs that Gibson has been making a bust of me. He wished it to be a surprise that the likeness might strike my friends at once, but I thought afterwards that it would please dear Mrs so to know of it that I made Henry tell her the secret in a letter of mine and now it is all out and so many people went to see it and it was so admired etc etc, and indeed it was most beautifully done.

Well it was finished, and the Caster came to cast the model, which cast was just finished, and all the pink of perfection, when some boys working in the place upset the stool on which it stood and the bust fell and broke to smash. What a thing! Poor Gibson was sadly disappointed, he had taken such pains with it, and done it so peacefully and you know the artists here don't take a cast from the face like Jackson but model it entirely from the eye, so it has all to be done … again; a work which took Gibson 3 weeks to model, and I have to sit again. However it is recommended and I expect we shall see it begun in marble before we leave Rome finally.

Did you hear of Gibson's present to me, a beautiful … in marble, Cupid and Psyche flying, it was there, not sold, in his studio, and we had asked the price which was £60, and one day to my great surprise he begged me to accept it, saying he would rather I had it than anyone he knew; indeed you have no idea how kind he is to me, and I am very fond of him and go everyday to the studio. I often talk to him about you dearest Emmes, and wish he could see you. I am copying a bust now, which I think resembles you, and I like so to do it and think of you as I go on.

The Carnival is now going on in Rome and such a row (to use a polite expression) I never beheld. It began on Tuesday and the general routine of the day is this: …Henry went last night with the Yates', we and they had taken a box in the theatre from which to see the fun. But I did not go - E. Bostock put on a Domino and Henry Mr Saunders's mask, and E.B. was mistaken for me, and they had the greatest fun I can't tell you in a letter, but I was ready to die of laughing when I heard of it all. Williams was therecin a black maskcand an old cloak, and she looked like the Diablo. I saw the pelting out of a window in the Corso, and I thought the people (English and all) were the greatest fools I ever beheld.

The carriages were full of bon-bons half time and the gentleman and all whitened over. I was coming along the street with H and Mr Gibson and a little sharp man, dressed up in a mask with a long nose and a fool's cape, came dancing up to me and swore (in French) that I had torn his heart, and he was dying of love for me, and I could hardly stand or look for laughing and Henry and Mr. Gibson were amused beyond measure. We could not get him away, for it is a kind of licenced impertinence in these times. How you would have laughed to see the soft thing skipping about me, and me hiding myself behind Harry! At last he vanished…A great many people have left for Naples but Rome is still full. We intend to leave here on Monday fortnight (the 25th) when time for these rooms is out, then go to Naples, come back in a fortnight to Rome and then 'hurray for home' after taking another look of farewell of this place which we have enjoyed so much. I shall be grieved to leave my kind friend Gibson but delighted to turn my fare homewards. … Dearest, dearest Emmes, I wish you looked (and I know you do) as well as me. My cheeks are quite rosy. I can walk miles…[12]

*Naples to Rome
March 8th 1839*

My dearest Emmes,

…If you had been standing by me this evening when we reached here, on the balcony of our room overlooking the sea, you would have believed all the delightful visions of fancy, poetry or prose, concerning Italy, were realised for the moment. I wished for you dearest Emmes! It had been a wet day, but the mists, save those of coming twilight, were cleared away. The wind was hushed, and the sea calm, and its waves came sweeping in, with a gentle rushing sound. Beneath my feet were the richest orange groves, in full bearing, and the flowers already in blossom, and their fragrance perfumed the air deliciously…we saw a good deal and above all Pompeii. We had seen before in the Museum at Naples the collection of things taken from Pompeii during the excavations - articles of common use, very much resembling those used at the present day - such as vases, jugs, plates, pans for cooking, etc and what is still more curious the very eatables, in a state of preservation, such as honey, flour, milk, eggs, bread in loaves (with the bakers name stamped on one), corn, rice etc. The eggs really struck me as most curious, to think such fragile things had been preserved for near 2000 years! I suppose the insides were petrified, they looked as natural as if Phaysan Garner had laid them… We set out to Pompeii about half past 9 in the morning on the 2nd March. It is 14 miles thro' an unpleasant road; very dusty and in a kind of street through suburbs, all the way… They drive like mad in Naples and we flew, in this little carriage, at such a rate I longed for you so, dear Emmes, I can't tell you, when we got to Pompeii and begun to walk through those deserted streets, and examined the houses once so gay and perplexed, of this 'City of the dead'.

Detail of Margaret Sandbach bust. Photographed by Antonia Dewhurst. Private Collection.
Blaen penddelw Margaret. Ffotograff gan Antonia Dewhurst. Casgliad Preifat.

[12]Centre for Buckinghamshire Studies, D115/10/61. Margaret to Edward Henry Roscoe, Rome, 8th February 1839.

It presents exactly the appearance you would imagine from knowing that the upper stories are entirely destroyed. Many parts of the houses, especially the baths, bed chambers and the shops, are very perfect and give an excellent idea of what the place once was. Still it appeared rather more ruinous than I had expected. - We walked about for nearly 3 hours, and I was so interested I did not feel tired. Then we took some nasty luncheon in a room belonging to the public baths, after which I made a slight sketch but with some difficulty, as the custode objected very much saying no one was allowed to sketch there…Oh how delighted I am that the time is coming and when we get our letters tomorrow. If they only bring good accounts of dearest Mrs, and of you (which God grant) I shall then feel quite happy. As the time draws nearer I grow more impatient and now I am so much better able to travel than I was when I first came to Italy. Henry is quite sleepy now, but he wanted to write a bit to make you laugh about me; I found a picture of some chicks in the room at Mola and I ran and did 'Tuck tuck tan' before it in great style, and when I turned around the waiter was in the room. The man must have thought me demented and Henry was ready to 'boson' and I looked very soft I dare say…[13]

Tuesday 23rd April 1839

Dearest Emmes,

… We arrived here last night at seven o'clock, exactly 3 weeks after leaving Rome, and having seen a great deal by the way and oh Emmes, such an exquisite road, tho' such scenery! Grand and beautiful beyond description, and some part of it quite exciting; being a great part of it, along the mountains on the coast, where the precipices are steep and the roads without protection of railing or parapet walls, so if a house had backed or the drag chain broke, or any catastrophe of that kind, we should have rolled into the sea in no time. Oh the beautiful blue sea with its glittering placid surface, the orange groves and olive woods, the far blue mountains, and the sweet little bays sweeping these fertile shores so lovingly. 'Love! Sons of Earth! For love is Earths' soft love. Look where ye will, earth overflows with me. Learn from the waves that ever kiss the shore, and the winds nestling on the heaving sea!' There is a lovely spot on the way to Genoa, the Bay of Spiaggia. We stayed there one night; a band of musicians came to serenade us, and as I listened to the pleasant music, and looked out upon the clear heavens glittering with a thousand glorious stars, I felt again as on that sweet evening at Mola that I was in Italy, the only land that can breathe around us such spells of enchantment…We were in a great flight at the Custom House entering France, Henry having presented me with a dress of Genoa velvet and we did not know till just entering that it is prohibited in France. I fully expected it would be taken from us, but the officers only examined the outside of the carriage, imperials etc and we had taken the velvet inside with us - wasn't it lucky…I forgot to tell you dear Emmes that Gibson modelled me on horseback before I left Rome, and he tells me in his letter that the sketch is cast, 'and has been seen by several ladies, and by Mrs Ingram and Lady Rob … who all admired it, and thought it quite new in sculpture'.

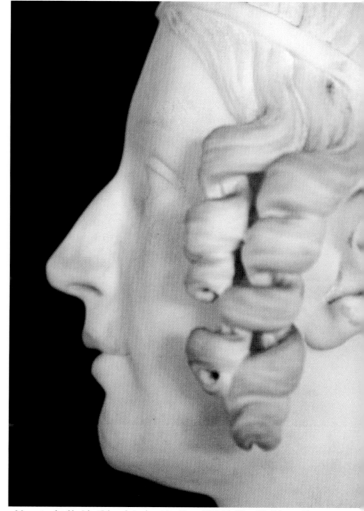

Margaret sculpted by John Gibson during her visit to Rome 1838-39. The original clay model was accidentally smashed and Margaret had to sit again for Gibson. Photographed by Antonia Dewhurst. Private Collection.

Penddelw Margaret wedi'i gerflunio gan John Gibson yn ystod ei thaith i Rufain 1838-39. Chwalwyd y model clai gwreiddiol yn deilchion drwy ddamwain a rhaid oedd i Margaret eistedd yr eilwaith i Gibson. Ffotograff gan Antonia Dewhurst. Casgliad Preifat.

Opposite: Watercolour painting of the French Coast by Margaret. Private Collection.

Gyferbyn: Paentiad dyfrlliw o arfordir Ffrainc gan Margaret. Casgliad Preifat.

[13]Centre for Buckinghamshire Studies, D115/10/69. Margaret to Edward Henry Roscoe, Naples and Rome, March 8th 1839.

31

Drawing of Heidelberg Castle dated July 12th 1838 by Margaret. Private Collection.
Lluniad o Gastell Heidelberg gan Margaret, dyddiedig 12 Gorffennaf 1838. Casgliad Preifat.

Opposite: The Last Adieu, goodbye to Gibson and Europe, dated 1839. Private Collection.
Gyferbyn: The Last Adieu, ffarwelio â Gibson ac Ewrop, dyddiedig 1839. Casgliad Preifat.

Sonnet on leaving Italy

Beneath the light of thy cerulean sky,
Fair Italy! no more my feet shall stray;
Far from thy verdant shores I bend my way,
And breathe for thee a fond and farewell sigh,
And count thee with the gems of memory!
Oh fragrant land of beauty! thou hast breathed
New life into my spirit — thou hast wreathed
Around my heart flowers that shall never die,
Like the brief things of earth, but evermore
Fed by the sunbeams of remember'd joy,
A radiance o'er the future hours shall pour,
That Time can never dim, nor Grief destroy —
For this I bless thee! On thy balmy air
I raise for thee a silent, parting prayer.[15]

It was his own fancy to do it. He models horses beautifully, and in his studio is a fine Arab he modelled from life. I have a great deal to say to you dearest on a subject most interesting to us both; but it will be better to talk than write about it. Perhaps dear Mrs mentioned to you Gibson's generous offer to execute for us some elegant tablet in memorial of our dear father for the Chapel. I had long wished for something of the kind and finding I did, he made this kind proposal, that we should pay for the marble and he would execute the sculpture. I can never repay his kindness in various ways and it seems to give him such pleasure to do anything for me…[14]

Paris
Friday 17th May 1839

Dearest Emmes,

…I fear you will think we are lingering very long here, but we thought it was best to take the opportunity of seeing Paris and most unfortunately the best thing worth seeing here, the Galleries of the Louvre are closed for a month! So we can't see them… I do so hate the steamboat and it makes my head so bad that my heart has failed me. I have been very well indeed here. Until last night when I was taken rather poorly. I think it was a little cold, and over excitement for I had been going about a good deal. After I came in from walking, in the evening I felt very tired, and I lay down rather sick. Then I got very feverish and my head bad, so Henry sent for the Doctor rather in a fright. He came directly - ordered my feet in a hot water, and a fever medicine, and a cup of warm tea for I had been shivering all over. I went into a great perspi and got a bit of nice sleep, and after a few doses of the medicine felt quite better, and when the Dr. came this morning he found me comparatively well and said I need take no medicines, but a nice warm bath this afternoon. I got up and I am very comfortable in the parlour, almost as well as usual. It was an odd attack, my pulse was 120 and every pulse in my body throbbing. He said I might go out again tomorrow and he would come 'en ami' to see me on Sunday. He is a nice man; a Scotch man… I am taking the opportunity of writing to you dear Emmes as I sit by myself, Henry having gone to the Chamber of Deputies - I suppose you have read all about the 'little revolution' here, it was very serious while it lasted, and a great many lives lost. (I forgot to say, speaking of the Dr. that he advised a short, in preference to a long passage, for he said it was bad for my head and I was grateful. Having asked him if I might go on Monday and he said oh yes - that I should be quite well tomorrow) …Well at any rate I shall soon be with you dearest Emmes, and we will have an excursion to Richmond and some spree there, and sit on the hill, overlooking that beautiful woodland scene, for a more beautiful one of the kind I have not seen in my travels and we'll dine at the Star and Garter…
…Dear Emmes I shall have a yellow face when I come out of the Boat, for I'm sure to be sick!!!!!!

Sunday… Goodbye for a few days dearest Emmes! I am quite disappointed to set off tomorrow - Henry sends his love.[16]

[14]Centre for Buckinghamshire Studies, D115/10/60. Margaret to Edward Henry Roscoe, 23rd April 1839.
[15]Margaret Sandbach, 'Sonnet on leaving Italy', Poems, (London: William Pickering, 1840), p.29.
[16]Centre for Buckinghamshire Studies, D115/10/68. Margaret to Edward Henry Roscoe, Paris, 17th May 1839.

M Bryce 1820

The last adieu

III

Havodunos

'Far from cities and from strife, Here we pass our rural life…'[1]

Inspired by their first encounters with Gibson, Margaret and Henry returned from Italy, back to their marital home, Hafodunos.

Dychwelodd Margaret a'i gŵr yn ôl o'r Eidal, i'w cartref priodasol, Hafodunos, wedi'i llwyr ysbrydoli yn dilyn ei chyfarfyddiad cyntaf â Gibson.

The name Hafod-unos is said to have been given by the circumstances that the formal train of Saint Winifred rested here for one night (un nos) on its way from Holywell to Gwytherin, a little village 4 miles distant, where the saint is said to have been buried.[2]

The macabre story of St Winifred casts a long shadow over Margaret's home at Hafodunos and the surrounding area. Twelve centuries before Margaret's time, Winifred, the daughter of a local nobleman, refused the advances of an amorous suitor, preferring instead to take holy orders and enter a convent. Her piety provoked a fierce rage in the man, who beheaded her. Her uncle, St Beuno, united Winifred's head and body and brought her back to life. At the spot where her head had fallen, a spring sprung forth and this became one of the most holy of pilgrims' destinations throughout the medieval period. Religious imagery of Winifred clearly shows the wound where her head had once been severed.

Five hundred years later, Winifred's bones were taken to a specially built shrine at Shrewsbury Cathedral. The monks entrusted with the passage of the holy relics came to a secluded spot at nightfall and set up camp on the site of Hafodunos, which is roughly translated to 'summer dwelling for a night'. Or so the story goes.

Taflodd hanes erchyll y Santes Wenfrewi gysgod hir dros gartref Margaret yn Hafodunos a'r ardal gyfagos. Ddeuddeg canrif cyn amser Margaret, gwrthododd Gwenfrewi, oedd yn ferch i uchelwr lleol, gynigion cariadus gŵr ifanc a phenderfynu bod yn lleian a byw mewn lleiandy. Parodd ei duwioldeb i'r gŵr golli'i dymer yn llwyr a'i dienyddio. Llwyddodd ei hewythr, y Sant Beuno, i ailgysylltu pen a chorff Gwenfrewi, a daeth hi'n fyw yr eildro. Yn y man lle disgynnodd ei phen byrlymodd ffynnon a ddaeth yn gyrchfan i bererinion drwy'r Canol Oesoedd. Mae delweddau crefyddol y Santes Wenfrewi yn dangos yn glir y clwyf lle torrwyd ei phen.

Bum canrif yn ddiweddarach, cludwyd esgyrn y Santes i Eglwys Gadeiriol Amwythig lle y lluniwyd creirfa arbennig ar eu cyfer. Treuliodd y mynachod oedd yn cludo'r creiriau sanctaidd un noson mewn man diarffordd. Galwyd y lle hwnnw yn Hafodunos neu 'preswylfa am un noson o haf'. Dyna'r hanes, beth bynnag.

Illustration of St Winifred's Holy Well by William Callow, 1866. Watercolour with pen and grey ink and graphite. British Museum.

Lluniad o Ffynnon Sanctaidd y Santes Wenfrewi gan William Callow, 1866. Llun dyfrlliw, gyda gwaith pen ag inc llwyd a graffit. Yr Amgueddfa Brydeinig.

Opposite: Moses Griffiths captured in watercolour the whitewashed house during the 1770s for Thomas Pennant, showing a building that had born the scars of its history well, including blocked-up windows, Georgian extensions and a reorientation of entry so that one would have no longer entered through the multi-storeyed porch. National Library of Wales.

Gyferbyn: Darluniodd Moses Griffiths y tŷ gwyngalchog yn ystod y 1770au ar gyfer Thomas Pennant. Mae'n dangos tŷ sydd wedi goroesi trafferthion y gorffennol, ffenestri wedi'u blocio, estyniadau'r cyfnod Sioraidd a mynedfa newydd fel nad oedd rhaid bellach defnyddio'r cyntedd aml-loriog. Llyfrgell Genedlaethol Cymru.

[1] Margaret Sandbach, 'Our Garden (Hafodunos): A sketch from nature, for a little friend', Aurora and other poems, (London: Pickering, 1850).
[2] MS M/D/SAND/4/4

The staircase from old Hafodunos. Originally, there would have been a first floor great chamber, which during Margaret's time served as a drawing room. The interiors were richly finished with panelling and an elaborate Jacobean staircase with flat splat balusters and carved strap work which resembled leatherwork. Private Collection.

Grisiau'r hen Hafodunos. Yn wreiddiol, byddai siambr fawr ar y llawr gyntaf oedd yn barlwr yn ystod cyfnod Margaret. Yn addurno'r tŷ roedd paneli pren moethus a grisiau Jacobeaidd coeth oedd â balwstrau ag estyll canol fflat a strapwaith cerfiedig oedd yn debyg i waith lledr. Casgliad Preifat.

Roedd Margaret yn gyfarwydd â'r chwedl. Wrth iddi orwedd yn effro gyda'r nos, gan geisio dod yn gyfarwydd â'r crecian a'r gwichian yn ei chartref newydd, gall hi'n wir fod yn cofio am boenau a duwioldeb y Santes Wenfrewi.

The legend of Winifred was well known to Margaret. As she lay awake at night, growing accustomed to the creaks and groans of her new home, she might well have pondered the pain and piety of Winifred.

My home now however differed from my former one in situation and resources and extent, possessing within itself more beauty, but not looking on such a wide-spread landscape as I have before described. Situated at the head of a little dingle, and nestled in trees the old house stands – it might almost be called 'the house with the seven Gables'. It is very old and when almost falling down was repainted not in a manner consistent with its antiquity and therefore lost something of its remarkable look. This dear old house is surrounded on the sides by garden and pleasure ground – the fourth side is built against a rock. It is said that many years ago some fine old oak trees were cut down by a former proprietor… One yet remains, a vulnerable tree, called 'the philosophers oak'. His magnificent grey trunk is now hollow, but he still spreads his green branches in the spring time, and seems to renew his youth. In the centre of the garden near the house stands a group of magnificent yew trees, whose grateful shade in summer and rich green foliage in winter make them always delightful. They are a source of constant amusement also from the circumstances of their being frequented by all sorts of birds, from the dove down to the golden crested wren. The birds build in the old stems of these trees, in storeys as it were in flats like the people in Edinburgh.

I have seen the beautiful nest of the golden crested wren hang, a mossy hammock, suspended under the branch, and the little birds six in number, sitting in a row above the nest when first they leave it, fed by their parents, waiting, tiny creatures, until they are able to take their first flight. In spring the woods are vocal with the various song cries of the Birds, the cooing of the dove, the chatter of the jay, the call of the cuckoo…[3]

Prynwyd Hafodunos, oedd yn blasty mawreddog o'r ail ganrif ar bymtheg ar gyfer y pâr ifanc yn fuan wedi'u priodas gan dad Henry. Roedd â'i gefn at y bryniau er mwyn ei gysgodi rhag y glaw a'r gwyntoedd gerwin. Roedd blaen y plasty ar ffurf E ac yn mwynhau golygfeydd dros y caeau a'r dyffryn gwyllt ger llaw.

The Hafodunos bought for the young couple by Henry's father soon after their marriage was a large early-seventeenth century mansion, situated with its back to the hillside so as to protect it from harsh winds and rain. The E-shaped front overlooked meadows and the uncultivated valley below.

Roedd Henry oddi cartref yn aml, gyda'i waith yn Lerpwl a Llundain. Dros dreigl y blynyddoedd, dioddefodd Margaret ei phoenau ac unigrwydd Hafodunos heb gwmni na diddanwch plantos.

Henry was often away on business in Liverpool and London. As the years passed, Margaret suffered the pain of her condition and the isolation of Hafodunos without the comfort and distraction of children.

[3]MS M/D/SAND/4/4

Nevertheless, Margaret grew to feel an attachment to Hafodunos, which was to strengthen her for the rest of her short life.

The garden in particular brought her much pleasure, collecting and cultivating the grounds and turning them into a paradise high up in the Welsh hills. In fact, the remoteness and detachment of Hafodunos from life proved to be an attraction, with visits to London limited to special occasions, such as John Gibson's sporadic returns to Britain. For Henry and Margaret's families, both based in and around Liverpool, Hafodunos was close enough for relatively frequent visits.

Er hynny, daeth hi i deimlo hoffter tuag at Hafodunos a ddaeth hyn yn gefn iddi yn ystod gweddill ei hoes fer.

Cafodd fwynhad arbennig o'i gardd, gan gasglu planhigion, meithrin y tir a chreu paradwys fechan ym mryniau Cymru. Daeth unigrwydd a phellter Hafodunos o fywyd beunyddiol yn fendith iddi gyda'i hymweliadau â Llundain wedi'u cyfyngu at achosion gwir arbennig, megis ymweliadau prin John Gibson â Phrydain. Gan fod teuluoedd Henry a Margaret yn byw yng nghyffiniau Lerpwl roedd Hafodunos yn ddigon agos ar gyfer ymweliadau achlysurol.

Our Garden (Hafodunos)

A sketch from nature, for a little friend

FAR from cities and from strife,
Here we pass our rural life;
Here, enclosed in mountain nook,
Read we Nature's varied book.
Here our garden's flowery ground
Spreads a loved enchantment round;
Lawn and stream and fountain clear,
Yew tree's shade, in summer dear;
Border trim, and Terrace walk,
Where we stroll, or sit and talk, —
And the winding ways that lead
To the woods or to the mead, —
Oh this pleasant garden ground,
What a charm it spreads around I
Here, the Rhododendron bed
Shows in Spring its brilliant red;
Rich and rare, of Eastern birth,
Nursed in our ambitious earth;
There, beside the murmuring brook,
Azaleas light and lovely look;

Daphne's fragrance scents the air,
And their stems the Lilies rear.
Here are pinks so small and sweet,
Flower mine eye delights to greet, —
Favourite flowers I a gift to me
From one we never more shall see.
Roses spread their welcome bloom,
And their own unique perfume;
Sulphur pale, and blush, and white,
Damask, moss, and crimson bright:
Roses, how we love them all,
Fairy low, and climber tall
Grey old gable, wreathed with these,
Standing out 'mid sheltering trees,
Dons his summer coat, and wears
Gayer smiles with growing years.
Seated in our Laurel bower
Where Clematis her starry flower
Mingles with the shining leaves,
And wild Hop its garland weaves;
Here we muse, and catch the light
Straying o'er the garden bright,

Through branches dark of ancient Yew,
Of stately growth, and sombre hue, —
We hear the birds from shady bough,
Chaunt their music sweet and low;
On the Fir-tree's spiral height
See the shining blackbird light,
Straining his expansive throat,
With that long delicious note, —
And I think, no miser's gold
Clutched within his eager hold;
Student's hard-won, longed-for prize,
Spread before his weary eyes;
Fame and state and fair success,
All the world calls happiness —
No, nor Izaak Walton's love
For his darling banks of Dove;
The Poet's for his Poplar Trees,
When he woo'd the summer breeze, —
Could be pleasure half so sweet
As we within our garden meet.[4]

It was my happy fate after the lapse of many years to return to the land of my early love, and deeper measure those beauties of nature and charms of rural life, which had flown almost into a passion with me.

The woodpecker tapping the beech trees, the flute-like song of the thrush, the deeper melody of the blackbird, and the little undertoned sweet warbling of a thousand little songsters. The harmonies blend with other harmonies of nature, with the fall of distant water, and the quiet ripple of the Rhan-hir stream, with the 'wave and hush again of the ever haunted woods', the bleating of the sheep, and the contented lowing of the cattle from the sunny hill side. Sometimes too with the many voices of children going or returning from school. Down the wood all thick and gay with wild flowers, then through the fruit and kitchen garden and a short distance along the road you come to the village with its little parish Church and church yard with the usual adornment of an old Yew tree - it faces you as you go down the road, and a green hill rises behind it at no great distance. I was walking down to the village one day in the spring – there had been a heavy shower, and a beautiful and striking scene met my eye as I approached the church.

4 Margaret Sandbach, 'Our Garden (Hafodunos): A sketch from nature, for a little friend', Aurora and other poems, (London: Pickering, 1850), p.127-9.

Front of the old Hafodunos. Entering through the new main door, one have would entered the long, low hall, with a great fireplace placed opposite the door. Two cross wings joined at either end, with parlours on the ground floors. It is probable that the staircase opened up at the rear of the hall, rising to the upper floors. Private Collection.

Blaen yr hen Hafodunos. Wrth fynd i mewn drwy'r drws ffrynt newydd byddai ymwelydd yn cyrraedd cyntedd hir, isel gyda lle tân enfawr gyferbyn â'r drws. Roedd dwy adain groes ym mhen draw'r cyntedd, gyda'r parlyrau ar y llawr gwaelod. Tebyg bod grisiau i'r lloriau uwch yng nghefn y cyntedd. Casgliad Preifat.

There was a funeral – and under the old yew tree a dark group of mourners had gathered around the grave – a gleam of light fell upon the spot – a rainbow made a bright arch above, and the misty shower was fading away on the hills. Earth and heaven seemed blended then – the dark group below – the brightness above. It was perfectly calm too, and not a sound disturbed the solemnity of the scene.

From the village with its scattered houses, its one comprehensive shop, an excellent little inn, the road branches off in these directions following the course of these streams. The Elwy is the principle one which flows down through a most beautiful valley, winding along meadows, now lost beneath steep banks, shaded by thick woods, now gliding out into the open country for perhaps half a mile, a clean rippling trout-stream. Travellers very seldom see this beautiful vale of the Elwy. Nothing can exceed the beauty of some points of view you hap along. It is fourteen miles from our village Llangernyw to St Asaph where the Clwyd falls into the Elwy. St Asaph takes it's Welsh name from the river and is called Glan Elwy – the other rivers are tributary to the Elwy and are called the Gerwyn and the Gledwyn. The Gledwyn comes from the gills of Gwytherin, through a very picturesque little vale or dingle, of which I have heard an artist say, that it would make his fortune if he could stop the river's flow and study. These little valleys are dotted with farms – and the buildings being scrupulously whitewashed every year, gleam out from overshadowing banks and woods and look bright and cheerful.

41

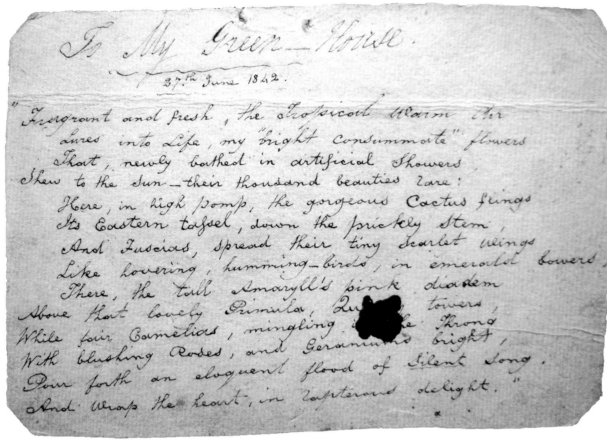

To my Greenhouse, a poem written on June 27th 1842 by Margaret, based on her adoration of her flowers. Private Collection.

To my Greenhouse, cerdd a ysgrifennwyd gan Margaret ar 27 Mehefin 1842. Fe'i hysbrydolwyd gan ei hoffter mawr o'i blodau. Casgliad Preifat.

Winter and Spring

Spring
I'm coming! I'm coming! the glorious Sun
Tells that my struggle with Winter is won!
Winter
Home again! home again! to thy bright bowers!
This is no time for thy sunshine and showers.
Spring
The flowers are calling me from the green sod,
To breathe on the scenes where thy footsteps have trod;
I hear their light voices in harmony say,
"Come, for our presence bids Winter away."

Winter
I'm not to be startled away by a flower,
Or by the soft threatenings of one sunny hour;
I'll unsheath my icicles, scatter my snow,
And bid the cold blast of the north wind to blow!

Spring
I defy thee to rob me of one of my flowers!
I mock thy stern glances, and laugh at thy powers;
Send thy bright icicles—I'll send my beams,
And melt them away with my warm sunny gleams.
Stay not my progress o'er the fair earth,
I'm coming, to welcome its glorious birth!
I will not go home again to my bright bowers,
Now is the time for my sunshine and showers!

Is given alone to thee?[5]

[5]Margaret Sandbach, 'Winter and Spring', Poems, (London: William Pickering, 1840), pp.37–38.

I think it is Wordsworth in a play on the scenery of the Lakes who speaks of the particular beauty of the grey stone, as harmonising with the tone of natural colouring. I have often noticed this harmony in Wales especially in wild parts of the country where everything is built of the native stone. Nonetheless I love the little white farms and cottages looking so clean and hospitably inviting – they are a kind people in our country and a slice of bread and drink of milk with a hearty welcome always awaits you at these little domiciles – following the stream of the Glegwyn, through up from Llangernyw, through the dingle I have described, you come to the village of Gwytherin, a place which makes one think of the scotch expression 'the back of beyond', you seem indeed to have reached the world's end, and yet in that as picturesque a spot as nature in her happiest moments ever spread before your eye. We generally leave the stream and approach the village from above, for the sake of the view. I will describe it as I saw it on coming, when we had been overtaken by a mountain mist and expected to see nothing. The mist cleared away – from the little hill on which we stood, the whole of the picture lay in sweet repose at our feet. This was the little dilapidated church almost a ruin with the magnificent yew trees in the church yard, making a map of dark shadow which told well among the bursting green of young summer grey cottages of the most picturesque form and proportion with blue peat smoke rising from the old chimneys - the dear stream winding away from the village down the valley, the cattle standing in the road to be milked. These were the new objects, while beyond the valley stretched in sweet fertility and on each side rose sheltering hills which shut in this lovely picture. To add to the effect of this moment, some children coming from school were singing as they went, and their voices sounded sweet and clean and happy.

But go on a little further and enter the village – doubly picturesque does it seem with its primitive inhabitants arrayed in such garments as Artists delight to paint - the children with pitches on their head, the old woman milking the cows - but such an impression of poverty, neglect & dejection among the aged meets you at every turn that you almost forget the natural beauty to mourn over the state of human beings so abject.

There are two decent houses but one whole street or row of houses has fallen down - no attempt is made to build, to repair, or to ameliorate the condition of the people, and I turn homeward with a sigh from my visit to Gwytherin, and willingly would give all the beauty and natural attraction it possesses for a hope of better things for the people. I need scarcely say that they are wretched poor, and come to their cottage doors and look at the stranger with something imploring & piteous in their look - an exception of this however I saw in a very jolly old woman, leaning against her doorway, while a friend of mine an Artist made a full length portrait of her. She was greatly flattered and elated.

A watercolour sketch of a Welsh cottage by Margaret. Private Collection.
Braslun mewn dyfrlliw o fwthyn Cymreig gan Margaret. Casgliad Preifat.

Hafodunos: Antonia Dewhurst

Summer and Autumn

Autumn

Fair flowers! Green verdure! O'er your bright display
I come to breathe the spirit of decay.

Summer

Not so, not so! Stay yet awhile our doom,
Touch not our beauty—sigh not o'er our bloom!

Autumn

I will but blend with it a softer hue,
And sprinkle o'er thy leaves a silvery dew,
And throwing o'er thy vest a richer light,
I'll make thee still more beauteous to the sight.
Thou canst not live eternal, then, oh why
Shouldst thou regret so sweet a death to die?

Summer

Away, deceiver! Through thy smile I see
A lurking tear, befitting such as thee;
Beneath thy chaplet rich, a glance so stern,
That from thy gaze most fearfully I turn.
Thy promise fair thou wouldst ere long betray;
Soon should I perish by thy hand — away!

Autumn

I will not leave thee—here I take my stand,
O'er thy domain I wave my russet wand;
Nought can avail thee—thou wert born to die,
Like all things fair and earthly—wherefore sigh?

Summer

Thou hast not conquered yet! Before thy rod
I bend not; on this bright and verdant sod
Thousands attend my call; soon will I raise
Voices to combat thee, and sound my praise.
I call you from your home, ye radiant flowers,
And tuneful birds, I call you from your bowers!
All ye who love your guardian Summer, come,
Unite your powers, and drive th' usurper home!

Autumn

In vain, in vain! Mark, on yon fading leaf,
The token that thy closing reign is brief;
On yonder flower behold a sparkling tear,
Autumnal dewdrops on its leaves appear;
They are my children now! Fair Summer yields,
She flies the forest and the verdant fields.[6]

[6]Margaret Sandbach, 'Autumn and Summer', Poems, (London: William Pickering, 1840), p.111.

David is a self-taught carver in wood; an interesting and intelligent creature, crippled from the hips downward, and in delicate health. So secluded is his position here that I think I was the first lady he ever saw - from his infirmities he cannot go about - specimens of his work were brought to us many years ago by a cousin of his who lived with the family - there was a sort of rude uniformity about them, which showed that the talent might be improved. We brought him from Switzerland some patterns, which he copied exactly and which suggested other work to him - we have since endeavoured to induce him to copy natural objects, such as foliage, which might give him originality to his designs, and he got the first prize at the Eisteddfod at Rhuddlan in 1850 for the best carving. He is now patronised by many kind friends able and willing to help him and he makes a very respectable living. He has built himself a little house and whenever you go there you find him sitting in the same corner all alone, with his little table and his tools before him. The bright smile with which he greets you is a full reward for the somewhat toilsome journey.

The most beautiful of all the walks and drives about Hafodunos we have not yet described, and it will be difficult by any description to bring before the mind's eye a picture so raw in beauty and varied in interest.

Ascending the hill about a mile above the house, you pass through improved land, planted and fenced until you come out upon the wide common, which stretches towards Llanrwst and Conway.

We pass one or two little farms or cottages, in one of which an accident happened a short time ago - the death of a little girl under the following touching circumstances. The child was about 5 or 6 years old - she had been left in the cottage by herself - she had seen her elder sister go with a brush to the back of the grate to get soot to black her shoes; following her example, she leaned over the embers and her little clothes which were thin and poor, caught fire - little is known of the child's suffering at that moment, but when her mother came in sometime after, she found her sitting on a little stool by the door quite naked, much burnt and in a state of great agitation but able to tell her what had happened. Her little half burnt clothes she had put into a pan of water, which showed singular presence of mind and sense in so young a child. The mother immediately sent for the doctor. He said he might have saved her life from the effect of the burns, but her nervous system had received a shock from which it could not rally. She fell into convulsions and died that night. The same night the mother was prematurely confined, but the baby lived and was called after the lost one, Catherine.

Speaking of cottages there is a poor family on the way to Gartherin, called 'Gors', who were all born blind. The old mother a respectable pious woman. Dr Lloyd Williams of Denbigh operated upon them and restored some degree of sight to two of them. One of these fell into bad company and was tried for horse stealing and theft – the other who travels the country with his donkeys was said to be engaged in questionable activities and in league with the poachers – but however that may be he has reformed and carries on a blameless trade, fetching coals for his neighbours and thus contributing to the support of his blind brother and half-blind sister. He goes by the name of 'Will of the Gors'. I met him continually in my miles over the mountain, plodding alongside his laden donkeys to one side, and greets me with a loud monosyllable 'Well...' – no more ever passes Will's lips.

It was an effecting sight to sit with them in their little cottage – the mother a pious and gracious woman now blind herself, who had suffered much not only from the affliction of her children but from the misconduct of her son, sat in the chimney corner. Robin, the eldest, stone-blind standing against the wall would very seldom turn his face to me – he was one of the most distrustful objects I ever saw, apparently suffering much from the sense of blindness. The sister a wonderfully active woman considering her affliction and very respectable, was busy making oat cake, and poor Will wondered in and out, not seeming to like visitors so much as his mother and sister did. But these simple and afflicted people were happy. The mother had the comfort of knowing before she died that her prodigal son had taken to better ways. She lay on the bed blind suffering and poor for some months, and I have been told by the vicar and his lady who often visited them that they had never seen an instance of greater piety and patience. A trifling thing was a great want to them. One pleasant spring day they had heard the cuckoo for the first time that year. It seemed to delight and cheer them – afterwards they all fell to talking about what they had been doing when they heard the cuckoo. 'Well Robin' said the mother, 'and what were you doing?' 'I was just scratching the cow' said Robin gravely.

…So might we say of the view from green terrace on the way to Llanrwst. I have named it 'the green terrace' by way of distinction, as there are so many points of view which we admire. The common on which we stand, which stretches like a green terrace above the lower common, is nibbled by the sheep to a close velvety turf. The position is high and the view extends like a panorama all around. In the middle distance are the beautiful rich colours of the heathery common, sweeping away into a soft blue – on the right a reach of the river Conway and the distant sea. To the left are picturesque undulations of ground, one on two little farms and a little grove of birch trees, and in the distance on that ridge are beautiful hills, gentle in the undulations and not less lovely than the grand Snowdon Range that meets the eye direct in front and in the crowning glory of our scenery. Oh beautiful and glorious mountains! How I have dwelt on you in eye and heart, till very speech and meaning seemed to come from your misty shadows, and your gleaming lights, how you have gladdened and cheered and elevated my soul, by your grandeur! Or sometimes by your perfect and indescribable peace: One winter evening (7th December 1850) when I saw you like purple monuments stand against the opal sky, no flitting light disturbing the scene serene no breath of wind uttering one mountain sigh, you spoke to me of the deep peace of the grave, and the glory of immortality, of the steadfastness of all the God's providence cried the truth and beauty of our faith which trusts in him.

Then again when the morning light played around your beautiful bows, what images of gladenings we saw in you! What tempting path for climbing your sides! What refreshing waterfalls and pleasant hills! And as we gazed from 'the green terrace' on your rugged sides, we planned many an excursion and strong limbed our enjoyment in the midst of you. Snowden rises predominant among the mountains. To the left in Moel Siabod a nearer mountain at the back of Capel Curig, which therefore looks one of the most important. It is a very graceful shape, and is exceedingly like Mount Socrate in the plain of Rome. The group includes of the rest of the Snowdon Range the Glydyr and Moel Airian, Carnedd Llewellyn and Carnedd Dafydd, stretching towards the town of Conway. This is on the road to Llanrwst. About 3 miles further on the whole way

Snowdonia: watercolour scene by Margaret. Private Collection.

Eryri: golygfa mewn dyfrlliw gan Margaret. Casgliad Preifat.

commands the most beautiful and picturesque views, especially as you approach Llanrwst and catch the windings of the river Conway, along one of the most beautiful valleys of North Wales.

The view we have been describing is seldom seen by tourists, for the roads are bad and lead across the country, out of the way of frequented tracks and runs. But it is well worth anyone's while who is travelling in Wales for the love of scenery to spend a few days in this district.

These were Margaret's last words, put down during the first week of June 1852, only a few weeks before her death.

Y rhain oedd geiriau olaf Margaret, a ysgrifennwyd ganddi yn ystod wythnos gyntaf Mehefin 1852, rai wythnosau cyn ei marwolaeth.

IV

'...the whisperings of superior spirits, they breathe to you and I...'[1]

Profile of Margaret by Gibson. Photograph by Antonia Dewhurst. Private Collection.
Proffil Margaret gan Gibson. Ffotograff gan Antonia Dewhurst. Casgliad Preifat.

Nod Gibson oedd cyrraedd y perffeithrwydd Groegaidd ym mhob model. Roedd wynepryd Margaret yn union yr hyn a geisiai mewn dynes. Roedd nodweddion ei hwyneb cymesur, lluniaidd fel duwies, ac yn ysbrydoliaeth gyson iddo yn ei weithiau diweddar. Cafodd Margaret ei hanfarwoli ganddo dro ar ôl tro mewn brasluniau a cherfluniau marmor gan iddo gadw'r prydferthwch ifanc a welodd cyntaf ym 1838 cyn i effeithiau afiechyd ddechrau dangos. O'r holl gerfluniau a gomisiynwyd ar gyfer Hafodunos, yr un a enynnodd y sylw mwyaf oedd Aurora. Dyma un o weithiau gorau Gibson a'r ysbrydoliaeth i gerdd fwyaf nodedig Margaret. Daeth hi yn fywgraffydd, ysbrydoliaeth a chyfaill mynwesol i Gibson; ei gyfraniad yntau oedd ei hannog i ysgrifennu a rhannu ei deimladau celfyddydol mwyaf dwfn gyda hi.

Gibson sought the Greek Ideal in every model; Margaret's form was everything he desired in a woman. With her balanced facial proportions, chiselled and goddess-like, her looks were to be a constant source of inspiration for his later works. He immortalised her in sketches and in marble over and over again. Preserving the young beauty he first encountered in 1838 before the ravages of illness took their toll. Of all the statues commissioned for Hafodunos, Aurora provoked the most intense activity, resulting in one of Gibson's best works and Margaret's most noted poem. She became his biographer, confidante and muse, whilst he reciprocated with encouragement for her writings and an invitation to share his deepest artistic thoughts.

[1]Aberystwyth, National Library of Wales, MS 20566E-25. John Gibson to Margaret, 25th January 1842.

Aurora by John Gibson. Photographed by Antonia Dewhurst. National Museum Cardiff.

Aurora gan John Gibson. Ffotograff gan Antonia Dewhurst. Amgueddfa Genedlaethol Cymru.

Rome
25th January 1842

My dear Mrs Sandbach,

Lear delivered safe the manuscript book to me.[2] Yes we shall be together there. My handwriting will be with yours. All these beautiful bits, these productions of genius are the whisperings of superior spirits, they breathe to you and I, beauties which we each feel, as you read and write them, so I read and feel them, my heart tells me so, but they purify my thoughts and bind me to you and to my art, in my art what do I feel, what do I encounter? Happiness, love which does not depress me, difficulties which I do not fear, resolutions which never abate, flights which carry me above the crowd, ambition which tramples no one down. I send you my grateful and affectionate acknowledgements from your little room where I am chalking up on the slate my new subject, Venus reproving Love for attaching himself to fortune. This idea amuses and pleases people much…

A few days ago Thorvaldsen was in this room of yours with the Baroness Stampe, his friend, whom I mentioned to you. She brought me back your little volume and said flattering things. He looked at your bust, said, 'who is this.' I told him. He turned to the Baroness, said, 'you see at once that this is a head of talent.' It is lucky you are not here just now for I fear that you would be flirting with Thorvaldsen and she would be jealous of you and I should be jealous of him and your husband would settle us both. He said to me, 'you should go to England and take the place of Chantrey.'[3] Said I, 'which place do you think I could produce the greatest works, Rome or London?' 'Oh Rome, Rome,' said he. 'Then why should I go to London?' 'to make a great fortune' said he – 'fame is my ambition not a fortune. I think, Cavaliere, that no one can produce works for lasting fame out of Rome.' The Baroness jumped up with fire flashing from her bright black eyes and said 'I differ with you. Thorvaldsen modelled now in his own country as fine things as he has done in Rome. Rome is a place to learn your art.' He interrupted her, and said, 'oh we are always learning.' I said to Thorvaldsen that we had been friends for many long years and that I often wished to possess a sketch on paper by him. He then said, 'most happy,' but told me that he had not a single drawing to give, turning round to her saying 'she robs me of everything in that way.' Then I told the Baroness if she would give me one of his sketches that I would make a drawing for her and she agreed and said she would be delighted. The small model of the Aurora stood by us and he looked at it long, considering it and I with the feelings and submission of a scholar to a great and venerable master of the art said I pray you to consider it for me and as usual say at once if it be worthy or not to be done in large. His sentiments were most encouraging and 'by all means do it full size' said he.

[2]Edward Lear (1812-1888) artist, author, and poet famous for his nonsense poetry. The manuscript referred to probably contained poetry for the collection included at the end of Giuliano de'Medici (1842).
[3]Sir Francis Leggatt Chantrey (1781-1841), leading sculptor of Regency England, who specialised in portraiture.

[Penry] Williams and the Baroness are making love. At a party the other evening they were sitting together in the corner and she called to Thorvaldsen who was sitting next to me and said 'Why Williams says he has began the picture for me'. He lifted up his hands in the air and said 'Oh what it is to be a woman.' It is two years since I gave him a commission and I have nothing yet but promises. Thorvaldsen is a great admirer of the works of Williams.

I am sorry that you have lost your grandpapa whom you liked so much. Our Doctor Gloage is going, we expect him to die tonight. It is consumption. He is a good man and clever and was always kind to me. We are all on the road, those who have just gone have past us but we are following fast. Before I go I wish to finish the Huskisson, the Hunter and to make a large group the design which I have had by me for some years.[4] Thorvaldsen has given me every encouragement to do it large and also before I go I wish to kiss your dear hand.

So you have begun a poem but you do not mention the subject. Now I shall not tell you the subject of my poems in future, however, I would rather not know it till I read it. …I am always intending to write down for you an account of my beginnings in the arts as you requested. Wyatt did not like England as a place for art and he was sadly disappointed with the state of sculpture there.[5] Chantrey's works disappointed him, he says he has no Greek feeling therefore falls into clumsiness and is graceless in his drapery, always bad and tasteless and this was the man who always preached against Rome as a bad school, persuading all young men not to go there. If this did not arise from a jealous feeling, who can deny that it did not arise from the narrow prejudice; the confined notions of a home bred artist – but Wyatt admires his busts and said that a few of his best portrait statues are in simple and good attitudes. Goodbye – continue to think of your friend – write soon. Tell Mr Sandbach I wrote a business letter to him. I am preparing my iron works to model the Aurora. People who do not understand art are much pleased with the Shepherdess, they find in it repose and soft melancholy. I shall model her too.[6]

John Gibson portrait by his close friend and popular artist, Sir William Boxall.
Royal Academy.

Portread o John Gibson gan ei gyfaill agos ac artist poblogaidd, Syr William Boxall.
Yr Academi Frenhinol.

Gibson's first visit to Hafodunos took place during the summer of 1844:

Daeth Gibson ar ei ymweliad cyntaf i Hafodunos yn ystod yr haf ym 1844:

Gibson was with us or near us, for two months - he spent a delightful quiet time here. I fully enjoyed his society. His characters of genius become more beautiful the more they are known - and those who know him most intimately must also admire him most…[7]

[7]Margaret to Lady Smith, from Hafodunos, 22nd October 1844, Osborn Shelves d 148, Yale Beineck Rare Book & Manuscript Library, Connecticut.
[4]William Huskisson (1770 -1830), British politician and Member of Parliament for Liverpool.
[5]Matthew Cotes Wyatt (1777-1862), artist and sculptor, a member of the architectural Wyatt dynasty.
[6]Aberystwyth, National Library of Wales, MS 20566E-25

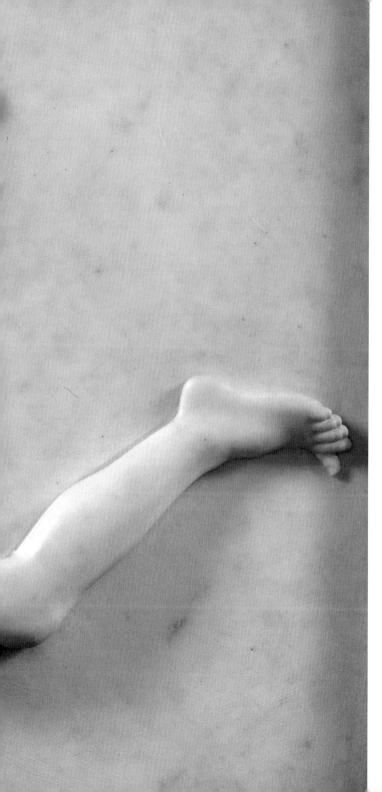

Cupid and Psyche

Behold, she flies thee, Love! with playful grace
Thy Psyche lures thee to the airy chase!
Securely thine she dares to leave thy side
In mock defiance, or in sportive pride.

She lures thee onward-through the yielding air
Flutter the light folds of her garment fair,
Through which her form, revealed in softened lines,
Upborne by wings celestial, purely shines.

And now with winning smile, she turns to thee,
Then leads thee onward still, with motion free,
And now she pauses, tempts thy warm embrace,
And then eludes thee, if thou win the race!

The summer sunbeams with their golden light
Are glancing on her braided tresses bright,
And with uplifted arm she holds on high,
Beyond thy reach, the captive butterfly.

But thou, young Love! on ardent wing hast flown,
And thy fond arms around thy Psyche thrown;
And while her face looks smiling down to thine,
The gifted sculptor traced your forms divine!

Thus may the soul, immortal, dwell with Love!
And range unfettered through the realms above;
Or calmly sleeping on his fragrant breast,
Taste all the sweetness of her heavenly rest.

Mortal! on earth thou mayst not sport with Love,
Thou know'st not the mysterius springs that move
His inward life, and thou in seeming play
Mayst wake a secret voice that urges him away![8]

Eros Pursuing Psyche, one of the first Gibson marbles purchased by Henry and Margaret during their trip to Rome in 1838/9. Royal Academy.

Eros Pursuing Psyche, un o'r cerfluniau marmor cyntaf i Henry a Margaret eu prynu gan Gibson yn Rhufain ym 1838/9. Yr Academi Frenhinol.

[8]Margaret Sandbach, 'Cupid and Psyche', De' Medici-A Drama-With Other Poems, (London: William Pickering, 1842), p.152-3.

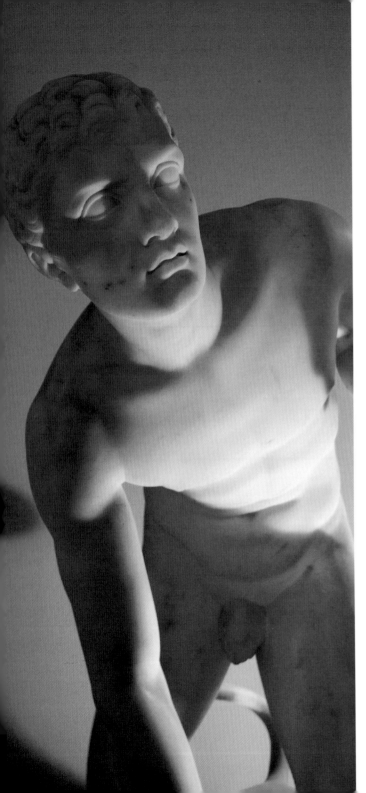

The Hunter and his Dog by John Gibson. Photographed by Antonia Dewhurst.
Private Collection.

The Hunter and his Dog gan John Gibson. Ffotograff gan Antonia Dewhurst.
Casgliad Preifat.

The Hunter and Dog

Youth, like the Sun, when high in his meridian
He has fulfilled the morn, and touches noon;
Beauty, the just proportion of each part
Borne to the whole, the Ideal formed of Truth;
Strength, nor gigantic, but so finely balanced,
Each nervous limb developing its power;
Grace, such as from consistent action comes,
The will and circumstances harmonious meeting;
Energy, that of manhood, when the mind
Presses its power upon it full-seen purpose,
And the firm body with a quick obedience
Follows it bravely, and achieves its will.

So stands the youthful Hunter, marble life;
In classic beauty true, and true to Nature;
He, like the conqueror of the Python, looks
Beyond himself, onto his victory,
Not won, like the bright god's, but yet to come,
And to his eye approaching. At his feet,
See, eager for the chase, with muscle strained
Against the arm that curbs him, the keen hound
In sight of prey, arrested as he springs
The man superior, stooping to control him,
And with raised brow, and eye perceiving, pauses
An instant on the issue. Thus he stands;
Repose and action centred in one point
Of time, eventful. And the Sculptor's genius,
Proved in appreciation of the moment,
As in its true embodiment, confessed,
Unchallenged, in his great work lives for ever.[9]

Gibson wrote to Margaret in 1841:

You must answer this, well what are you about, tormenting the soul. I must tell you what I am doing, modelling a sketch in clay for a new statue. If it should please me I shall put it into execution and you shall have the first offer. It is a subject that no sculptor here has done nor have I ever seen a statue of it. It is Aurora young and lovely. I represent her stepping from the waves of the sea upon the earth, one foot on the wave and the other on the flowers which do not bend with the weight of her 'The dew loves the flower and does not oppress them.' In her right hand is a vase out of which she pours the dew which she has collected from the sea and in the other she holds a young rose, 'the rosy fingered morn' with roses in her hand says Virgil and you see a star upon her head…[10]

Again he writes to another friend after the statue's completion:

Rome
4th November 1848

…I am anxious that you should see my statue of Aurora: when it is brought to Aigburth perhaps you will then see it. I think it is the most poetical single figure that I have done. It is an advantage when a statue has much about it that has a meaning. The name 'Aurora' is pleasing, and fills the mind with agreeable feelings. Aurora has one foot still touching the wave of the sea, and the other upon the earth; her head is adorned with stars – 'Mother of the Stars'; as she moves lightly onwards she scatters the dew from her urn. The stars are painted blue, and the ornaments of her dress delicate pink. But… I do not wish to bind you down to praise this work of mine. I have not yet made a work that I am perfectly satisfied with; still, I think this is one of my best…[11]

Ysgrifennodd Gibson at Margaret ym 1841:

Yna ysgrifennodd at gyfaill arall ar ôl iddo gwblhau'r cerflun:

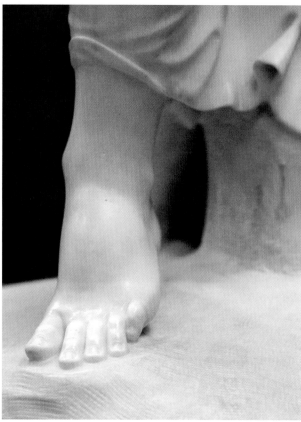

Aurora by John Gibson. Photographed by Antonia Dewhurst. National Museum Wales.
Aurora gan John Gibson. Ffotograff gan Antonia Dewhurst. Amgueddfa Genedlaethol Cymru.

[9]Margaret Sandbach, 'The Hunter and Dog', Aurora and other poems, (London: Pickering, 1850), p.11-12.
[10]National Library of Wales, MS 20566E-23. John Gibson to Margaret, 6th December 1841.
[11]John Gibson, Unpublished Letters, (n.p:n.d.), p.14.

Aurora by John Gibson. Photographed by Antonia Dewhurst. National Museum Wales.

Aurora gan John Gibson. Ffotograff gan Antonia Dewhurst. Amgueddfa Genedlaethol Cymru.

Aurora

Delicious Dawn! Up from the cradle bed,
*   Rocked by the old Ocean with low-lulling care,*
Awake she soars, her angel wings outspread,
*   That softly beat the dusky-dreaming air.*
Before the world his drowsy eye encloses,
*   She at her guardian's fountain fills her urns,*
And while the mighty sleeper still reposes,
*   To the glad East her course unerring turns.*
Hail to thee, chaste Aurora! See she flies,
*   The morning star shines pale upon her brow;*
Here is no dazzling glory; from her eyes
*   No glances flash, no streams of brightness flow.*
Calm, holy, steadfast, clear, and yet more clear,
*   The pearly light around her sweetly lies;*
And the grave heavens their virgin child revere,
*   And silent welcome smiles along the skies.*
Serene she moves – but in that silence deep,
*   She hears the unquiet Earth beneath her stir,*
And meets the thousand eyes, half roused from sleep,
*   That slowly turn their dreamy gaze on her.*

What hast thou seen, oh Maiden,
Upon this dim world, laden
*   With care and joy, and pain?*
From out its troubled surges,
Its songs and chaunts, and dirges,
*   What, Maiden, dost thou gain?*

Knowledge and wondrous learning;
And my deep soul is burning,
*   Eager to watch the strife.*
Each new day from my portal,
I see a struggling mortal
*   Start on the race of life;*

Some rushing up the mountain,
Some pausing at the fountain
*   To drink, and gather strength;*
The wise one, and the sad one,
The weary and the glad one,
*   All sink to rest at length.*

Men call me smiling Morning,
And paint my beam, adorning
*   The flowery meads of May;*
Few read my spirit duly,
And they who know me truly,
*   Speak me not blithe and gay.*

The life that breaths with me
Is solemn; none can win me
*   To jollity or mirth;*
Often with feeling fearful,
And eyes not seldom tearful,
*   I watch the suffering Earth.*

I hear the deep sighs bursting,
I see the dry souls thirsting
*   For love they cannot find;*
For hope and love, that started
Once with the tender-hearted,
*   And left them far behind.*

And joy which they inherit,
Who are touched with finer spirit
*   Than the many sons of clay,*
Full as briefly and as brightly,
As the dew I scatter lightly,
*   Flies ere its noon away;*

Oft beautiful and gifted,
And soaring high, uplifted
*   On Genius' radiant wing, -*

Keen as that thrilling gladness,
The sharpest pang of sadness
    Rings from the self-same strings.

I hear Death's awful fiat,
I mark the breathless quiet
    That sleeps upon the pall;
I see the deep grave hollowed,
I see the black bier followed,
    I hear Love's anguished call.

I watch the foam-clad Ocean,
Tossing in wild commotion
    The Bark upon its breast;
I touch the heaving billow,
That rolls above the pillow,
    Where many take their rest.

Down in unfathomed places,
Lie low those long-lost faces,
    That suffer a "sea change;"
Beyond imagination
That beautiful mutation,
    That "something rich and strange."

Down on the panting City,
With weariness of pity,
    My early glance I cast.
I meet the hymn ascending,
Of toil and grief unending,-
    Never the first, nor last!

The feet to labour going,
The weary fingers sewing,
    The haggard eye and frame;
Despair its last draught drinking,
The homeless wanderer sinking,
    And the bowed head of shame.

To these my soft light stealing,
The hopeless day revealing,
    Is but a boon unbidden;
Brings tears down wasted faces,
Fresh woe in woeful places,
    And the bowed head is hidden.

I have listened to the sorrow
That, morrow after morrow,
    Has wrung its hands in vain;
I have risen to hear cursing,
Remorse's wild rehearsing,
    The sinner's deadly pain.

I have looked into the Prison,
Where the convict has arisen,
    Upon his day of Death;
I have met the straining cry,
Confession's agony,
    And prayer's awe-stricken breath.

But Joy hath not departed
From Earth. The noble hearted
    Walk on beneath mine eye;
In the eternal quietude
Of duty, where no clouds intrude
    Between man and the sky.

I see the Pilgrim toiling,
With sword and armour foiling
    The Tempter and the Lion;
Straight by the Palace Beautiful,
Toils on the soldier dutiful,
On, to the hill of Zion.

Over Earth's roughest places,
With pale and gentle faces,
    I see fair women go;
While with a sweet regard
Their steps the Angels ward,
    And light around them throw.

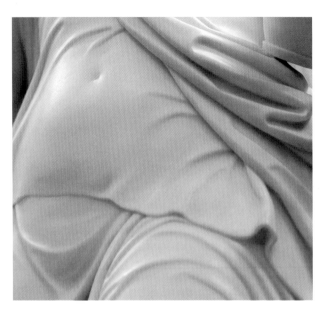

Some born to bliss and beauty,
On their bright way of duty,
    With genial impulse of spring;#
One long glad song of sweetness,
Tells of the spirit's meetness
    A heavenlier strain to sing.

From childhood's purest pleasure,
Lavished in largest measure,
    Such beings glide to youth;
From youth to life's full glory,
And old age calm and hoary,
    All vowed to love and truth.

My earnest soul rejoices,
To catch their happy voices,
    And blesses as it hears;
But there is triumph greater,
Though coming slow, and later,

And born of many tears;

The triumph of the Martyr,
Of him who will not barter
    His Soul for earthly good;
Whose holy heart is fixed,
Possessed of peace unmixed,
    In its strong solitude:

Whose faith is ever-living,
And knoweth no misigiving
    Because it is for God;
For God, and in Him, wholly,
Gazing high, kneeling lowly,
Crowned while beneath the rod;

The triumph of tried hearts,
When love with duty parts,
    And weeping, goes alone;
When, ere their last embrace,
Virtue stood in her place,
    And sacrificed her own;

While Passion bows before her,
No longer to implore her,
    But to confess, and die,
In mourning robes enshrouded,
Prostrate in dust, and clouded
    With tears of agony.

Peace-ministering Angels
Then fly with glad evangels,
    To meet the conquering soul;
In its divine foundation,
Unshaken by temptation,
    And 'mid the wreck, still whole:

The triumph of the Patriot,
Whose holy ardour waited not
    For promise, nor reward;

But in the Senate fearless,
And in the battle careless,
    His Country's foemen dared:

He who with great fidelity,
With pride, and with humility,
    Trusted the good in store;
Preached the great advent boldly,
And looked on caution coldly,
    And lived by faith the more:

The triumph of Love all spiritual,
Beyond all bond and ritual,
    Even the bond of duty;
For where Love guides supreme,
Right things and happy, seem
    One, in her heavenly beauty.

Then the soul follows free,
Elastic, joyfully
    Exults, unbound, new born;
The task God sends is light;
And toil becomes delight,
    And grief no more forlorn.

Yea, such the peace and gladness,
And glory 'mid the sadness,
    And Faith amid the fear;
From out those troubled surges,
And songs, and chaunts, and dirges,
    Such music do I hear.

Then the angelic Eos dropped her eyes,
    Her pale blue eyes, with heavenly tears o'er brimmed;
Her beauteous bosom heaved with gentle sighs,
    And a soft floating cloud her presence dimmed.
Sweetly emerging then, and lifting up

> Those lids, upon whose fringes hung her grief,
> Into a wakening Lily's ivory cup
> She poured cool dew, and on its wavy leaf.
> Awhile the distant breeze was heard afar,
> And clearer light gleamed in the Eastern skies;
> Upon her brow grew paler the pale star,
> Fading before Apollo's bright uprise.
> "Return, return! oh maiden pure and holy!-"
> Onward she fled away on snowy wing,
> That wafted back an air of melancholy,
> And seemed the flitting mists of thought to fling
> About the enquiring Spirit.
> Now shone the Day:
> The Ocean's golden waves danced in the beam,
> And Light flew laughing on her azure way;
> And mingling in a rich and odorous stream,
> The melodies of Heaven and Earth resounded,
> And Nature's heart with wakened gladness bounded.[12]

[12]Margaret Sandbach, 'Aurora', Aurora and other poems, (London: Pickering, 1850), p.1-10.

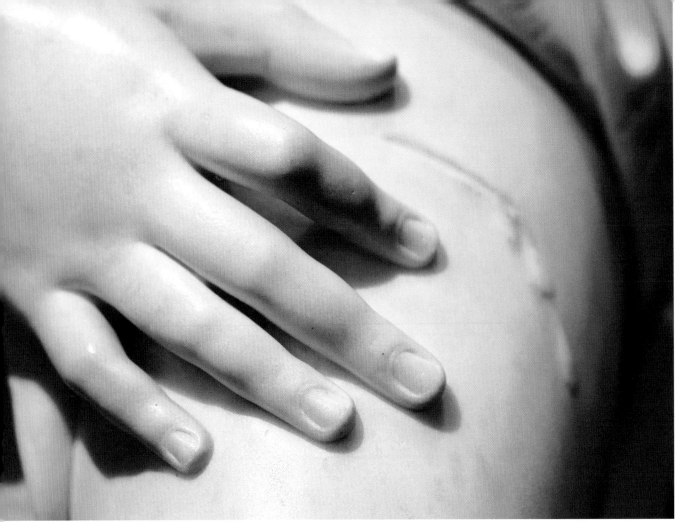

The Wounded Amazon by John Gibson. Photographed by Antonia Dewhurst. National Museum Wales.

The Wounded Amazon gan John Gibson. Ffotograff gan Antonia Dewhurst. Amgueddfa Genedlaethol Cymru.

The appeal of 'The Wounded Amazon'

And hast thou wounded me? ev'n thou, whose fame
To the admiring world I would proclaim!
Has thy hand pierced the limb so white and pure,
That ever stood in battle firm and sure?
Ah! canst thou look on me, and yet command
That thus for ever doomed to pain I stand?
Mark the glad vigour of my perfect form,
That bends in graceful ease, or braves the storm,
That fain would now pursue the wild career,
And pants to draw the bow, or hurl the spear!
My fair companions onward speed their way,
I hear a lingering voice, "Away, away!"
And I would spring to join the glittering band,
Yet fail, arrested by thy magic hand.

Art thou relentless?—then my task shall be
With gentle patience thus to yield to thee,
With generous love declare thy matchless skill,
And with thy praise the future ages fill:
Genius has stamped upon my shining brow.
The light of beauty, and I bear it now
Unfading and triumphant! —Though the wound
To one sad spot my fixed regard has bound,
Still shall the Amazon unconquered be,
And proudly claim the laurel wreath for thee![13]

[13]Margaret Sandbach, 'The appeal of 'The Wounded Amazon', Poems, (London: William Pickering, 1840), p.15-16.

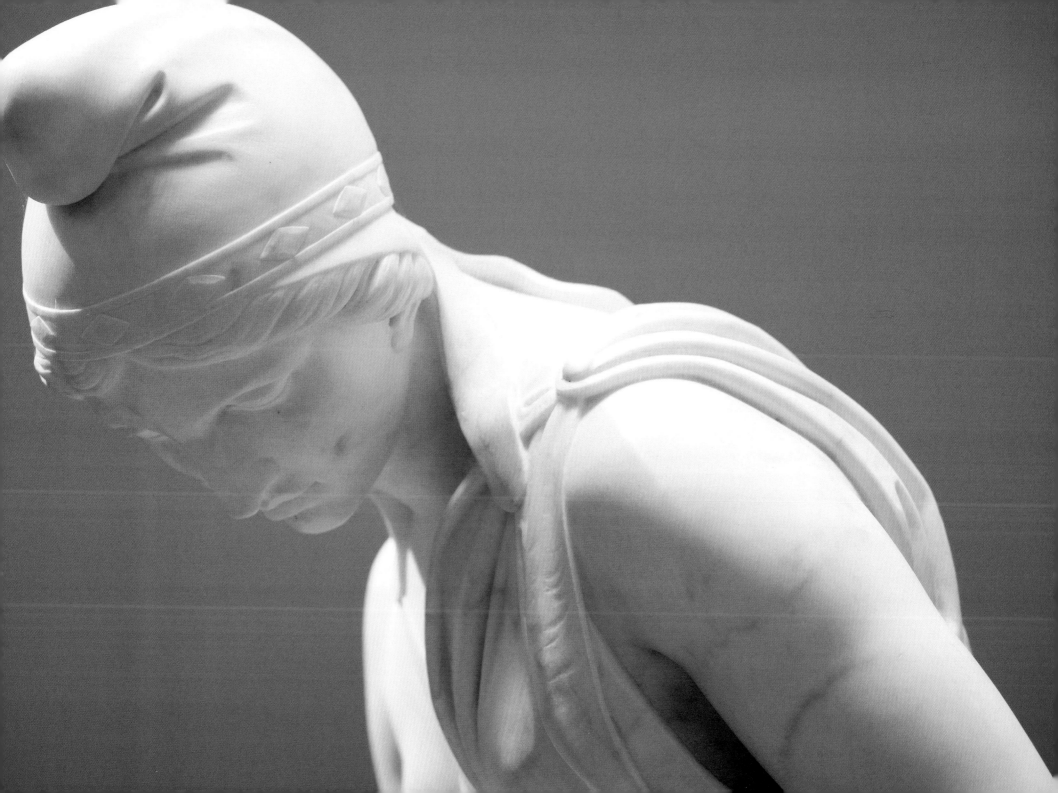

V

'These Poems are worthy of a daughter of Mr. Roscoe...'[1]

Cyhoeddiad cyntaf Margaret oedd casgliad o'i cherddi ym 1840 dan y teitl syml Poems. Roedd yr adolygiadau yn eithaf ffafriol, yn aml yn crybwyll ei llinach o William Roscoe oedd yn enwog iawn bryd hynny.

Margaret's first publication was a collection of poetical works in 1840, simply entitled Poems. The reviews were generally good, often referring to her descent from William Roscoe, whose fame was widespread:

'These Poems are worthy of a daughter of Mr. Roscoe. They are distinguished by the correctness and elegance of the composition, the sweetness and tenderness of the thoughts, and the grace and beauty of the images and descriptions.'[2]

Ym 1843 cyhoeddwyd Giuliano de'Medici - A Drama - With Other Poems a gafodd adolygiadau llai ffafriol. Y tro hwn ceisiodd Margaret ddilyn arweiniad ei thaid drwy ddramateiddio rhan o hanes y teulu Medici. Roedd William Roscoe wedi gwneud enw iddo'i hun fel hanesydd drwy gofnodi hanes y teulu yn Life of Lorenzo de'Medici ym 1796. Defnyddiodd Margaret gyfrol ei thaid fel sail i'w cherdd ddramatig oedd yn disgrifio'r chwyldro yn Firenze pan lofruddiwyd Giuliano (1453-1478), brawd ieuengaf Lorenzo, a'i gyd-lywodraethwr yn Firenze. Yng ngeiriau un adolygydd 'Mrs Sandbach is an ambitious person. Being the grand-daughter of William Roscoe, she believes that she lineally inherits all that was his, and gives to the world her tragedy and poems… We fear she will stand alone in this agreeable delusion…'. Anadlodd fywyd i gymeriadau hanes ei thaid, ond tynnodd yr adolygydd cyfoes sylw at foneddigeiddrwydd y cymeriadau o'i gymharu â grymuster trigolion Firenze a dialogau mwy brathog Shakespeare.

In 1843, Giuliano de'Medici - A Drama - With Other Poems was published, to somewhat less favourable reviews. This time Margaret attempted to directly follow her grandfather's lead by dramatising part of the Medici story, which William Roscoe had notably recorded in his 1796 Life of Lorenzo de'Medici, which earned Roscoe a reputation as a historian. Margaret used her grandfather's tome as the basis for her dramatic verse on the Florentine revolt which surrounded the assassination of Lorenzo's younger brother, Giuliano (1453-1478), his co-ruler of Florence. One reviewer stated that 'Mrs Sandbach is an ambitious person. Being the grand-daughter of William Roscoe, she believes that she lineally inherits all that was his, and gives to the world her tragedy and poems… We fear she will stand alone in this agreeable delusion…'[3] She breathed life into the characters from her grand-father's history, yet the contemporary commentator remarked at the politeness of the characters in contrast to the forcefulness of Florentines, comparing Shakespeare's more vitriolic dialogues.

[1] Unknown, 'Review of Poems', Gentleman's Magazine, October 1840, pp. 408-9.
[2] Unknown, 'Review of Poems', Gentleman's Magazine, October 1840, pp. 408-9.
[3] Unknown, 'Giuliano De' Medici -A Drama-With Other Poems', The Morning Post, February 1843.

Margaret was inducted into the Academy of Arcadia at Rome, and she dedicated the poetry section of her 1843 book to them. The waspish remarks continued insinuating that the Italian members were 'famous judges of lovely women, though of a lovely woman's English verse they be as ignorant as Spanish mules…' They state that the complexity of language was confounding and though she was 'not bound to write intelligible poetry… she should certainly speak intelligible English.'[4]

Another play followed in 1845, albeit published anonymously, entitled The Amidei: A Tragedy in Five Acts (and in Verse), this time following another Florentine family, the Amidei, this play tells the tragic story of orphaned siblings, Laura Amidei and her older brother Count Amidei. They are joined together by an intense bond, reflecting no doubt, Margaret's relationship with Edward Henry. Owing greatly in theme to Shakespeare's Romeo and Juliet, this tragedy was viewed more favourably than Giuliano de'Medici.

Daeth Margaret yn aelod o'r Accademia degli Arcadi yn Rhufain, a chyflwynodd adran y cerddi o'i chyfrol 1843 i'r aelodau. Parhaodd y sylwadau bachog oedd yn awgrymu bod yr aelodau Eidalaidd yn 'famous judges of lovely women, though of a lovely woman's English verse they be as ignorant as Spanish mules…'. Y farn oedd bod cymhlethdod yr iaith a ddefnyddiai yn drysu'r darllenydd ac er nad oedd hi'n 'bound to write intelligible poetry… she should certainly speak intelligible English.'

Ysgrifennodd ddrama arall ym 1845, yn ddienw'r tro hwn, yn dwyn y teitl The Amidei: A Tragedy in Five Acts (and in Verse), y tro hwn yn dilyn teulu arall o Firenze, yr Amadei. Hanes trist brawd a chwaer amddifad, Laura Amidei a'i brawd hynaf y Conte Amidei sydd yma. Mae perthynas gref a grymus rhyngddynt, sydd bron yn sicr o fod yn atgof o'r cwlwm clos fu rhwng Margaret ag Edward Henry. Gan fod y drasiedi hon i raddau yn adlewyrchu Romeo a Juliet gan Shakespeare, roedd yr adolygiadau yn fwy caredig na rhai am Giuliano de'Medici.

The Cottage, Aigburth, in the grounds of Woodlands, was Margaret and Henry's Liverpool home. It had been formerly a farmhouse built around 1700 out of sandstone. The later additions, such as the gabled end, were built out of brick and then plastered over. Margaret's sketch shows the house during the late-1830s. Private Collection.

The Cottage, Aigburth, ar diroedd Woodlands oedd cartref Margaret a Henry yn Lerpwl. Bu'n dŷ fferm a adeiladwyd o dywodfaen tua 1700. Wedi hynny, adeiladwyd rhai gwelliannau, megis talcen y tŷ, mewn brics a orchuddiwyd â phlastr. Mae braslun Margaret yn dangos y tŷ yn ystod diwedd y 1830au. Casgliad Preifat.

The Cottage, Aigburth
25th February (1845?)

My dear Lady Smith
You are very kind to write to me as you do & it makes me happy to know that my pen work has pleased you so much & that the character of Laura I have endeavoured to describe met with your sympathy & approbation. I hope I have in some degree succeeded in giving expression to her character - but as a Tragedy I lament over many deficiencies it has. So you guessed it was mine? I had been trying to keep myself quite out of sight but many of my friends have discovered me & though I trust my name is yet a secret in the world of critics I find it is well known, or rather well guessed here.

It would be a very great pleasure to me, & an advantage to know what Professor Smythe thinks of it. Sometime or other, if you have heard him express any opinions. I have the highest respect for his judgement - veneration I may say…[5]

[4]Unknown, 'Giuliano De' Medici -A Drama-With Other Poems', The Morning Post, February 1843.
[5]Connecticut, Yale Beineck Rare Book & Manuscript Library, Osborn Shelves d 148. Margaret to Lady Smith, from Hafodunos, 27th March 1845.

A life size silhouette of Margaret made during her visit to Rome. Private Collection.

Silwét maint llawn o Margaret a wnaethpwyd pan oedd hi yn Rhufain. Casgliad Preifat.

Ni wyddys beth oedd teimladau Margaret am y beirniadu cyhoeddus o'i gwaith, ond teimlodd reidrwydd i beidio â defnyddio'i henw ei hun.

Margaret's private thoughts on the public criticism of her work are not known, but she felt obliged not to use her name:

Hafodunos
March 27 1845

My dear Lady Smith
Thank you so much for sending me the Professor's letter, it is a great pleasure to me to read anything of his, & it was very kind of him to take the trouble of writing all that long letter about my poor book which I feel is very unworthy of the thoughtful & friendly attention bestowed on it. I think I told you I had a most kind letter from Mrs Baillie & Sigr Talfourd has also been so good as to write about it to a mutual friend. This & the Professor's letter, with one or two others, I treasure highly, & feel that they make me independent of much public criticism which so far, with very little exception, seems be withheld. Indeed 'the Amidei' has fallen away harmlessly upon the world! and in the Country, as I almost always am, I should probably miss the sight of any passing notices in the public journals. I once thought it impossible that I could ever feel indifferent about this - but, I do now, so completely that I often forget it altogether. Oh the misery of those who have to write for bread or look for happiness from Fame - from the fickle breath of popularity…

I am very happy indeed to find that the 'Amidei' in any way pleases Professor Smythe - The subject was found fault with, also, by Sigr Talfourd and I am persuaded that it was an unfortunate one to select. It struck me on reading Sismondi's Italian Republics - & I did not properly consider & digest it before getting to work I found innumerable difficulties start up as I went on - but I had to conquer them - instead (as would have been better) giving up the subject. The rival feud may suggest some degree of likeness to the plot of Romeo & Juliet, but the position of the persons is so very different throughout, (the love entirely so, because the Hero does not really love the Ghibelline) that I cannot see how the idea of that beautiful play should go along at all with the perusal of mine - do you? Yet the Professor says so, & so, therefore, it may be. I never imagined it when I was writing… Your letter just caught me, on the wing for Wales & this is the reason I have not written sooner to thank you. We are come here now for all the year till next winter & I think I almost enjoy these few half busy, half idle, unsettled days - looking about here & there - searching for an early violet out of doors & arranging my little affairs in the old oak room - our favourite haunt. But soon I must settle down to proper ways. I have written to you during my interruptions…[6]

[6]Yale Beineck Rare Book & Manuscript Library, Osborn Shelves d 148. Margaret to Lady Smith, from Hafodunos, 22nd October 1844.

The now lost manuscript 'Recollections of my Childhood' was commenced about 1847, but never completed, together with Gibsonia, an unfinished biography of John Gibson which was to be used as the principal source for Lady Eastlake's biography in the 1860s. Gibsonia ends with a note dated October 1851:

Dechreuwyd ar y llawysgrif Recollections of my Childhood sydd bellach ar goll, tua 1847, ond ni chafodd hwn na Gibsonia, bywgraffiad o John Gibson eu gorffen ganddi. Defnyddiwyd Gibsonia yn brif ffynhonnell ar gyfer gwaith y Fonesig Eastlake yn chwedegau'r ganrif honno. Daw Gibsonia i ben gyda nodyn sy'n ddyddiedig Hydref 1851:

'Here, I regret to say, our conversations were broken off… And now I much fear that ill health on my part may prevent my pursuing a subject to which I have so long looked forward with hope and pleasure.' Gibsonia's current location is not known.

After reading 'The recreations of Christopher North'

CHRISTOPHER North!

'Through the sweet Poet-land we've walked with thee, By the lake side, o'er mount, and grassy lea,
With joyous feet
Met the young Morn, and hailed her Hebe smile,
 Or marked Eve's parting hues on fair Belle-isle,
Still led by thee.
On, further on, into the Forest deep,
 Where old Sylvanus and the Dryads sleep,
We went with thee;
 Till on the solitude a breath of gloom,
 For one dark moment whispering of the Tomb,
 Swept o'er the soul.

We were beside thee when thy startled eye,
 Flashed from the calmness of its reverie,
 From dreams of Heaven,
 And mysteries untold, — to see the Deer
 From hills of storm pursue his wild career,
 Through the green gloom.
We stood with thee upon that forest glade,
 Marked the blue violet nustling in the shade;
 And then, with thee
Followed the onward guidance of the stream
 Till all around us glowed the open beam
 Of sunny air.
We have been with thee in the halls of mirth,
 And sported with thee round thy father's hearth;
 Or wept with thee,

As the soft memories crowding on th'y brain,
 Gave to imagination power again,
 To see that home.
We have risen with thee on thy powerful flight,
 When thought pierced boldly to the realms of light;
 And when thy mind,
Like "the sun-starers," when they cleave the sky,
 Sustained its course, nor turned its dauntless eye
From the full blaze.
We have been with thee — it is over now,
 And thy rich spirit with its fervent glow,
 Guides us no more;
Here the dumb book, which we in sorrow leave,
 Fails in its sympathy, and cannot grieve
 With us, at parting![7]

[7]Margaret Sandbach, 'After reading 'The recreations of Christopher North', Aurora and other poems, (London: Pickering, 1850), p.114-5.

Cyhoeddodd Margaret ei thrydedd cyfrol o farddoniaeth Aurora and Other Poems dan yr enw Mrs H. R. Sandbach. Cyflwynwyd y gyfrol i Gibson oedd wedi ysbrydoli nifer o'r cerddi. Mae'r adolygydd yn dechrau â'r gerdd Conway ac yn nodi fod Margaret

As 'Mrs. H. R. Sandbach', Margaret published a third book of poetry, entitled Aurora and Other Poems. Much of the poetry was inspired by Gibson, to whom she dedicated the book. The reviewer starts out with the poem Conway, remarking that Margaret

'…has attempted the poetic treatment of the locomotive. Coke is a difficult subject to all but stokers and pokers. We cannot say that Mrs. Sandbach kindles any poetical impulse with the ashes of Shelley…
A beautiful statue of Aurora by Gibson furnishes a happier vein of inspiration. The artist has realised in marble a sentiment happily, if not very originally, cast into words by the writer:—

> *"Calm, holy, steadfast, clear, and yet more clear,*
> *The pearly light around her sweetly lies;*
> *And the grave heavens their virgin child revere,*
> *And silent welcome smiles along the skies."*

…Other works of Gibson's furnish subjects for several similar poems. Mrs. Sandbach has a fine eye for form. Gibson's 'Hunter and Dog' are set before us with spirit and elegance… But ever so many such graceful trifles don't make a good volume of poems; and we must see whether the muse do not reserve something better for us.'[8]

Sylw mewn adolygiad arall mwy cadarnhaol yw bod Margaret yn

A more positive review remarked that Margaret was

'…a poet; she has the true and holy gift, and, we would fain believe, in fuller measure than this volume betokens. Would that she would let her heart pour out unrestrainedly upon the subjects of her verse, but it is kept in and back by line and rule, and although she writes beautifully it is with an air of restraint…'[9]

Wedi'r adolygiadau deifiol ar Giuliano de'Medici, cyhoeddodd Margaret dair nofel yn ddienw: Hearts in Mortmain a Cornelia, dwy nofel mewn un gyfrol ym 1850, a Spiritual Alchemy: or Trials Turned to Gold ym 1851.

After the scathing reviews for Giuliano de'Medici, Margaret went on to publish anonymously three novels Hearts in Mortmain, and Cornelia, two titles sharing a single volume in 1850 and Spiritual Alchemy: or Trials Turned to Gold in 1851.

[8]Unknown, 'Aurora and other poems', Dublin University Magazine, 1850, pp. 573-574.
[9]Unknown, 'Aurora and other poems', The Gentleman's Magazine, August 1850, p. 174.

Critic Virginia Blain calls Hearts in Mortmain, and Cornelia 'probably the best of her several prose fictions.'[10] Hearts in Mortmain, is composed of a series of letters centred on a semi-incestuous passion between Ethel and Edward, a sister and brother. Cornelia's protagonist is an orphan, and later a singer, who is

Yn ôl yr adolygydd Virginia Blain, mae Hearts in Mortmain, a Cornelia yn debygol o fod: 'the best of her several prose fictions.'[10] Cyfres o lythyrau am berthynas led-losgachol rhwng brawd a chwaer, Ethel ac Edward yw Hearts in Mortmain. Merch amddifad sy'n tyfu i fod yn gantores yw prif gymeriad Cornelia a chafodd ei

'thrown when a girl into the way of the very being against whom her benefactress is the most implacable,—drawn towards him by a mysterious sympathy,—and only at the very last moment allowed to learn what he is to her and what she is to him.'

As to the identity of the author

Ynglŷn â phwy yw'r awdur

'the book before us is evidently written by a lady; and one of the most prominent characteristics of the present position of this branch of Literature, is the great extent to which it has fallen into the hands of women….To come to such writings as Hearts in Mortmain, and Cornelia, after the anxieties and roughness of our worldly struggle, is like bathing in fresh waters after the dust and heat of bodily exertion.'[11]

Again, to Lady Smith she enquires:

Eto mae hi'n gofyn i'r Fonesig Smith:

'Lady Smith, whether a book called 'Hearts in Mortmain & Cornelia' which came out last August has fallen in your way? I wonder if you read it & how you liked it. I did not give my name, nor did I wish it known as mine but it has crept out somehow or other, & now, it is no use making a search of it. I can hardly believe I did not send you my volume 'Aurora' last year - but I cannot remember its going though I am sure I intended it should. I therefore send it by the same post as this & by your acceptance of it, with much love. I have not written your name in it for I cannot be certain that a copy did not go to you through the Publishers.'[12]

[10]Unknown, 'Hearts in Mortmain, and Cornelia', The Prospective Review, 1850, pp. 494-511.
[11]Unknown, 'Hearts in Mortmain, and Cornelia', The Prospective Review, 1850, pp. 494-511.
[12] Yale Beineck Rare Book & Manuscript Library, Osborn Shelves d 148. Margaret to Lady Smith, from Hafodunos, 21st April 1851.

John Audubon, famed botanist, who helped inspire Margaret's interest in fauna and flora illustration. After the artist Cruickshank, dated 1835. British Museum.

John Audubon, botanegydd enwog oedd wedi ysbrydoli diddordeb Margaret mewn lluniau anifeiliaid a phlanhigion. Wedi'r artist Cruickshank, dyddiedig 1835. Yr Amgueddfa Brydeinig.

Cymharwyd Spiritual Alchemy yn wael â Hearts in Mortmain. Dywed The Westminster Review:

'It is of that class of religious novels which aim at a didactic effect by an inflated style of reflection, and by melodramatic incident, instead of faithfully depicting life and leaving it to teach its own lesson, as the stars do theirs.'[13]

Er hynny, canmolwyd y plot, y cymeriadau a dull yr ysgrifennu yn frwd gan adolygydd arall. Dywedodd bod y

'...story is full of interest, and it is, without overflowing, full of characters, all of whom are extremely well drawn. There is, indeed, one character, Passiflora, which may be pronounced a master-piece, and which must of itself set the author in no ignoble rank amongst our best and most popular novelists. There are scenes, in which this girl appears, wrought with extraordinary energy and passion, scenes which, once read, can never be forgotten. 'Spiritual Alchemy' is the production of a shaping and original mind.'[14]

O gyfnod ei phlentyndod, roedd Margaret wedi arfer cyfarfod â nifer o bobl bwysig a dylanwadol. Ond nid tan ddiwedd tridegau'r ganrif, wrth i'w henwogrwydd gynyddu, y gallodd hi fod yn gydradd yn eu mysg. Roedd y teulu Roscoe, er enghraifft, yn gyfeillion agos â Henry Fuseli (1741-1825), artist ac awdur y nodwyd ei ddylanwad gan William Blake. Yn Records of a Country House, mae hi'n dwyn i gof bod yr ymweliadau gan fawrion Lerpwl ar ddiwedd y cyfnod Sioraidd, yn ogystal ag artistiaid, actorion ac awduron wedi gadael argraff barhaol arni hi a'i brawd:

Spiritual Alchemy was compared to Hearts in Mortmain and paled in its shadow. The Westminster Review stated:

Yet another review raved about the plot and characters, the style of writing exclaiming that the

From childhood, Margaret had met many prominent and influential people. But it was during the late 1830s that her own star was in the ascendant and she could move in these circles as an equal. For instance, the Roscoes were close friends with Henry Fuseli (1741-1825), artist and writer, whose influence was noted by William Blake. In Records of a Country House, she recalled visits from the great and good of late-Georgian Liverpool, as well as artists, actors and writers, leaving an indelible impression on her and her brother:

'We were now brought into intimate and delightful intercourse with our Grandfather Mr Roscoe – that dear and remarkable grandfather, who was always so good and kind to us, and at whose house we were accustomed to see many interesting and celebrated persons, some of whom made a particular impression on our youthful fancy. Among them Audubon the naturalist became our favourite friend – he used to spend many hours with us, occupied in making drawings of those English birds not already added to his collection.

Among other people we saw at once Grandfather's I best remember Alexander the ventriloquist, whose powers excited our high admiration and wonder – he performed in the drawing room for our especial edification – Lord (then Mr) Brougham whose nose we considered his most remarkable point, and compared to our favourite rabbits, Mrs Hemans then in the zenith of her poetic fame and Professor Smythe of Cambridge of whom we were very fond. The professor was a charming old gentleman – full of animation and kindness and intelligence. Even then, child as I was, he influenced me as a man rather of cultivated and elegant mind, and extensive information, than of great original pennies. He was an intimate friend of my Grandfathers, and many a bright evening have we spent in their pleasant company. One peculiarity of the Professor entertained us very much, his intense love of strong tea, and quantities of sugar. I used to peep into his cup and see the sugar piled up standing out at the top. In his amusing little play called 'Lady Morley's Lecture' he says, Ladies do all things well but one and that is making tea, 'They spare the Caddy.'

Monsieur Alexander by Thomas Charles Wageman. Famed as a ventriloquist and general entertainer, here he is seen wearing a woman's dress and frilled cap, looking much as Margaret would have seen him when she was a child. British Museum.

Monsieur Alexander gan Thomas Charles Wageman. Yn enwog fel tafleisydd a diddanwr cyffredinol, yma mae'n gwisgo dillad merch a chap ffril, ac yn edrych yn debyg iawn i sut y gwelodd Margaret ef pan oedd hi'n blentyn. Yr Amgueddfa Brydeinig.

A drawing of Conwy Castle by Margaret. Private Collection.

Lluniad o Gastell Conwy gan Margaret. Casgliad Preifat.

Conway

THE virgin Moon is up in state,
The sea-waves wear her light;
Their calmly-measured motion breaks
The stillness of the night;
Upon the shoulders of the cliff
A shadowy pile is borne,
The Castle walls are grey with age,
Their bold support unworn.
And lonely there, on Conway's tower,
Turned to the East his face,
The hoary genius of the spot
Holds his time-hallowed place.
His mantle dusky with the wear
Of many hundred years,
His aspect firm, his withered eye
Dim with old age's tears.

But calm he stood in conscious pride
Serene, in silent power;
Wrapt in his thoughtful solitude
Waiting the passing hour:
The fair moon sunk; the Watcher still
Stood watching for the Dawn;
And soon across the East beheld
A band of crimson drawn.
But never Morn was ushered in
By light so red and bold,
And never on such air as this
Night's parting knell was toll'd.
Not the light step of flowery maid,
But Thunder's tread was there;
And distant shrieks and discord loud,
Broke on the vaporous air.
Nearer it glows, yon fitful gleam,
Nearer it comes apace,
Deeper the hoarsely echoed song

It sings upon its race.
It comes, it comes; a rushing cloud
Trailing its track of fire,
And heaving as with inward storm
Of hurrying desire.
And quietly the grey old Towers
Looked on—till burning light
Touched with strange glow the velvet moss
And the wall-flower on its height;
And there the watcher, druid-like,
Still stood, a dauntless form;
While round him gathered noisily
The fiery panting storm.
And through that cloud a vision passed
Of human hands upheld,
And brawny arms, that Vulcan-like,
All that opposed them, felled.
And from that fire there issued forth
A shape with flaming wings
And glowing eyes, and streaming hair,
And voice that sharply rings:

I am the daughter
Of Fire and Water,
Pursuing my iron path
Ever in haste,
For my course is chased,
By the breath of their mingled wrath.
Not in love, but strife,
They have given me life;
I sprang from their grasp in scorn,
I saw at my birth
An era for Earth,
And full armed for my work I was born.
O'er Earth arid o'er Ocean
Triumphant I lead,
The rock's gloomy Cavern

Has witnessed my speed.
Vesuvius' Volcano,
And Snowdon's grey crown,
On the track of my travel
Look wandering down.
Yield then, oh Ancient!
Thy Lordship to mine;
Men's praise and men's wonder
No longer are thine.
Fast in the mist of time
Fades thy faint power;
New light bursts around thee,
Thy empire is o'er.
Quick gathering vapours hid that aged form;
'Twas seen no more when passed the insulting storm.
But nightly when the winds and waves are still,
And holy silence broods o'er Tower and hill,
Is heard a chaunted dirge, low-voiced, and sad—
And seen, they say, a band of mourners, clad
In amice grey. With ivy wreaths, entwined
By loving hands, the hoary heights they bind,
With tender music they invoke the shade
Of the dead Past, whose glory, lowly laid,
Shall reign no more, whose high and ancient crown
By bold intrusive feet is trampled down.
Watch, ye who sought and loved that beauteous scene
While yet unspoiled it wore its charm serene,
Watch, wait, and listen. For that spirit band
Is seen and heard alone, by those who stand
Silent in loyal love, with saddest pleasure,
And hearts responsive to the tender measure.
For you they chaunt their solemn song, while sweet
The gentle echoes wake the psalm to meet;
For you this sunlight of the garish day
Shall melt in memory's softened light away;
And by her "lamp of beauty" you shall see
The lovely landscape as it used to be.[15]

Margaret had now taken her place in the ranks of women writers of her period. Britain, particularly North Wales, was dominated by the voluminous writings of Felicia Heman (1793-1835). Like Margaret, Felicia was born in Liverpool and moved as a child to Gwrych, near Abergele, where she published her first volume of poetry at age 14. Felicia wrote to William Roscoe, determined to be the main breadwinner for her family, after her father had been bankrupted in the Liverpool crash of 1793 and deserted his family. She raised over a thousand subscribers for her first collection of verse, among them Roscoe, who not only subscribed but also lobbied publishers, Cadell and Davies. Roscoe even oversaw Felicia's printing and wrote the preface. She continued her literary career on her marriage and was a well-respected author, praised by Wordsworth during her lifetime and after her death. Margaret must have seen many parallels with Hemans, even though she never achieved her level of fame.

Of all the influences on Margaret's life the greatest was John Gibson, whose connections and friendship circle, were opened to Margaret after her visit to Rome. Gibson introduced her to the Welsh artist Penry Williams (c.1800-1885), son of a stonemason and a house painter who was born in Merthyr but spent most of his life in Rome. He frequently returned to Britain and also to Hafodunos. On one of his visits to Britain, whilst staying with Mrs. Huskinson at Eartham in 1851, he sketched Margaret whilst she worked, capturing her role as an author, pensively sat at a desk, with papers spread.

Bellach, enillodd Margaret ei lle ym mysg llenorion benywaid ei chyfnod. Roedd gweithiau Felicia Heman (1793-1835) yn dylanwadu'n gryf ar Brydain, ac yn arbennig ar Ogledd Cymru. Fel Margaret, cafodd Felicia ei geni yn Lerpwl. A hithau'n blentyn ifanc, symudodd i Wrych, ger Abergele, ac yno yn 14 oed, cyhoeddodd ei chyfrol gyntaf o gerddi. Ysgrifennodd Felicia at William Roscoe, yn benderfynol o fod yn brif gynhaliwr ei theulu ar ôl i'w thad fynd yn fethdalwr wedi trychineb Lerpwl ym 1793 a gadael ei deulu. Casglodd dros fil o danysgrifwyr, gan gynnwys Roscoe, ar gyfer ei chasgliad cyntaf o gerddi. Rhoddodd ef air o'i phlaid i'r cyhoeddwyr Cadell and Davies yn ogystal â chadw golwg ar yr argraffu ac ysgrifennu'r rhagair. Parhaodd Felicia â'i gyrfa lenyddol ar ôl priodi a daeth yn awdures o fri. Yn wir, derbyniodd ganmoliaeth gan Wordsworth yn ystod ei bywyd ac ar ôl ei marwolaeth. Rhaid bod Margaret wedi gweld sawl tebygrwydd rhyngddi hi â Felicia, er na chyrhaeddodd hi byth mo'r un uchelfannau.

O'r holl ddylanwadau ar fywyd Margaret y pwysicaf oedd John Gibson. Roedd ei gysylltiadau a'i gylch cyfeillion ar gael i Margaret yn dilyn ei hymweliad â Rhufain. Cyflwynodd Gibson hi i'r arlunydd o Gymro Penry Williams (c.1800-1885). Roedd yn fab i saer maen a pheintiwr tai a anwyd ym Merthyr Tudful ond a dreuliodd y rhan fwyaf o'i oes yn Rhufain. Dychwelodd yn aml i Brydain ac i Hafodunos. Yn ystod un ymweliad ym 1851, tra roedd yn lletya gyda Mrs. Huskinson yn Eartham, brasluniodd Margaret wrth ei gwaith, gan ei darlunio'n awdures, yn eistedd yn feddylgar wrth ei desg ymhlith ei phapurau.

Felicia Dorothea Hemans by unknown artist, circa 1835. One of the most celebrated female poets of the early nineteenth century, Felicia was admired by the aspiring Margaret in her youth. National Portrait Gallery.

Felicia Dorothea Hemans gan artist anhysbys, tua 1835. Hi oedd un o'r beirdd benywaidd enwocaf ar ddechrau'r bedwaredd ganrif ar bymtheg. Edmygwyd hi'n fawr gan Margaret pan oedd hi'n ifanc. Oriel Genedlaethol y Portreadau.

15 Margaret Sandbach, 'Conway', Aurora and other poems, (London: Pickering, 1850), p.134-8.

Sir William Boxall (1800-1879) by Michel Angelo Pittatore, 1870. Boxall was good friends with William Wordsworth, John Gibson, Sir Edwin Landseer and also with Sir Charles Lock Eastlake, whose widow, Lady Eastlake, used Margaret's correspondence with Gibson to write his biography. National Portrait Gallery.

Syr William Boxall (1800-1879) gan Michel Angelo Pittatore, 1870. Roedd Boxall yn gyfaill da i William Wordsworth, John Gibson, Syr Edwin Landseer a hefyd Syr Charles Lock Eastlake. Defnyddiodd y Fonesig Eastlake, ei weddw, lythyrau Margaret a Gibson i ysgrifennu bywgraffiad Gibson. Oriel Genedlaethol y Portreadau.

Daeth artist arall o Gymru yn gyfaill mawr i Margaret. Roedd Mary Lloyd (1819-1896) wedi astudio gyda Gibson yn Rhufain. Ganwyd hi yn Llanbedr Dyffryn Clwyd, Sir Ddinbych ac roedd hi'n aeres i Stad Hengwrt. Bu hi'n byw am sawl blwyddyn gyda'r awdures a'r ffeminydd Frances Power Cobbe (1822-1904) gan efelychu Boneddigesau Llangollen. Cyfeiriai Margaret yn aml at Miss Lloyd yn ei dyddiaduron a'i llythyrau, gan sôn am ei hymweliadau â Hafodunos a'i hiechyd gwael.

Daeth Edward Lear (1812-1888) i adnabod y teulu Sandbach yn Rhufain, ac ymwelodd â Hafodunos gan sôn yn ei ddyddiaduron am y coed llawrydd a'r gwiwerod coch oedd yno. Gwnaeth Margaret gryn argraff ar Lear, gan gyfaddef 'that was a woman' ond ei bod hi'n dioddef 'spite of the foolish Dean sisters.' Saith mlynedd wedi marwolaeth Margaret, cyfarfyddodd ag Elizabeth Charlotte, ail wraig Henry, a'r sylw yn ei ddyddiadur oedd 'alas! Margaret S.!!'.

Cyfaill arall a gyflwynwyd i Margaret gan Gibson oedd William Boxall (1800-1879), y peintiwr portreadau oedd hefyd yn gyfarwyddwr yr Oriel Genedlaethol yn Llundain. Mae ei lythyrau at Boxall yn arbennig o ddadlennol a phryfoclyd, yn cyfeirio at gellweirio preifat ac yn fwyaf rhyfeddol, at gerdd wamal am Tennyson oedd yn destun sawl sylw brathog…

Another Welsh Artist, Mary Lloyd (1819-1896), a sculptor, who studied under Gibson in Rome, became good friends with Margaret. She was born in Llanbedr Dyffryn Clwyd, Denbighshire, as an heiress to the Hengwrt Estate and lived with feminist writer Frances Power Cobbe (1822-1904) for many years, modelling themselves on the 'Ladies of Llangollen'. Margaret frequently refers to Miss Lloyd in her diaries and letters, mentioning her visits to Hafodunos and often Lloyd's poor health.

Edward Lear (1812-1888) became acquainted with the Sandbachs in Rome, and visited Hafodunos, lovingly referring to the larches and red squirrels in his diaries. Margaret made a considerable impression on Lear, as he confirms 'that was a woman' but she suffered at 'spite of the foolish Dean sisters.'[16] Seven years after Margaret's death, he met Henry's second wife, Elizabeth Charlotte, but comments in his diary 'alas! Margaret S.!!'[17]

Another friendship made through Gibson's introduction was with William Boxall (1800-1879), portraitist and director of the National Gallery in London. Her letters to Boxall are particularly revealing and flirtatious, referring to private jokes and most extraordinary of all, a comedic poem on the subject of Tennyson, who received an acidic lashing...

8 April 1846
Hafodunos

Dear Mr Boxall

Here is the 'Lesser Celandine' - its golden star peeps out so brightly from the broken banks. Our banks are very rich, though they are broke – I don't mean a pun!

I believe Spring or something like it, is at hand at last - what a winter it has been! We had deep snow here a week ago - but now there is a fresh warm wind, and the thorn tree buds have dared to open.

How are you? I hope you never look back upon that wretched time at Aigburth except to rejoice in emancipation from such horrors. I have had a wretched cold since I came here - but am better.

We have letters from Gibson - he was finishing the bas-relief of the Hours and the Horses and quite engrossed with it. Ben, poor 'Mr Ben' - had been awfully ill but he hoped was getting better - a terrible tumour on his side and Gibson had been quite unhappy about him. He says Mr Ben is an excellent creature, too good for this world, but an obstinate beast when he's ill. It is such a droll letter - so characteristic - I was much disgusted to see in the paper that a Liverpool artist is to do Mr Holmes - for I don't believe theres a good portrait painter in Liverpool, setting aside all the hope we had that you would be the one. Perhaps the whole Committee will find themselves done, as well as Mr Holmes! Oh what a pun this time! I darest not write anymore for fear of marking another bad one so goodbye. Write to us some of these days. Alas! We are not coming to London this Spring. You must come here.

Believe me,

Yours affectionately,
M Sandbach[18]

Mary Lloyd of Rhagatt and Hengwrt, sculptress and assistant to Gibson, and near neighbour to Margaret in North Wales. Courtesy of Auriol, Marchioness of Linlithgow.

Mary Lloyd o Rhagatt a Hengwrt, cerflunydd a chynorthwyydd i Gibson. Roedd hi'n gymydog agos i Margaret yng Ngogledd Cymru. Trwy garedigrwydd Auriol, Ardalyddes Linlithgow.

[18]London, National Gallery Archives, NGA1/22/102. Margaret to William Boxall, 8th April 1846.

24th August 1846
2 North Parade
High Harrogate
This is our address at present

My dear Mr Boxall,

How are you? And did you find the weather any better in Liverpool and Cheshire than in our dear old Wales? I hope you will visit soon, for we are wishing much to hear from you. Did the box arrive safe in Liverpool? Here are some questions to answer, so you cannot make an excuse that you have nothing to say! It was very dull, in more senses than one, after you left us, at the station - it began to rain too and to enliven us a little, one of the old horses tumbled down, poor thing, and broke its knees on that bad road. This was our only event or adventure, and at night we went on to Birmingham, and next day through a most beautiful country to our brother's Rectory in Herefordshire, happily many miles away from any railroad. I thought of you as we passed by the fine wooded banks, and noble trees standing in majestic groups on the park-like meadows - or when we saw pretty children with their bright bold faces upturned to watch us pass.

It is in the Valley of the Teme, so rich and fertile - orchards and hop gardens and bowing woods. The Rectory is a very pretty old place - a lawn sloping to a brook, and a beautiful broken bank along the side - just what would please you. How I thought of all our pleasant strolls! Do you remember one day speaking to me of Mrs Cardwell and your poor sister and you said 'we must not talk of this anymore' and we went out? I was musing over it as we were travelling and wrote the enclosed which I venture to send you.

We are going some day soon to Bolton Abbey - I wish you were here to go with us! I shall try to sketch. Our windows here look to the west, and I have seen two glorious sunsets and wished I could look into the sun's eye as you can! But I long to be back at Hafodunos… Just as I was reading that passage about the insupportableness of the idea of Eternity, down rushed the Train into a long dark tunnel, with the most the most unearthly shriek you ever heard.

Believe me dear Mr Boxall,

Ever yours,

M.S.

After asking Boxall for Tennyson's autograph:

Ar ôl gofyn i Boxall am gael llofnod Tennyson, daeth y nodyn canlynol:

An amazon vanquishing a foe vanquishing a soldier in battle, pen and ink drawing by John Gibson. Private Collection.

An amazon vanquishing a foe vanquishing a soldier in battle, lluniad pen ac inc gan John Gibson. Casgliad Preifat.

'My dear Louis,

Many a poem of mine has perished because I was too idle to write it down. It is nausea to me to re-write what is printed. Excuse me therefore. This will serve for an autograph. Give it to the Lady.

Ever yours,

Alfred Tennyson'

Margaret's response to Tennyson's note:

Dyma ymateb Margaret i nodyn Tennyson:

It was not worth your while! Oh honest Poet!
Honest and lazy - nor ashamed to show it -
So I take that for truth which you have writ,
Pleased with the spirit that indicted it!

Tis a voluptuous day - the birds are singing -
And nature to the Poet's heart is bringing
All that he wants - all that he cannot make
Much that he cannot give and yet will take -

I should have been so grieved to make you sick,
By troubling you from your old stores to pick,
A verse or two to suit a begging lady -
A gem to shine with a place so shady!

Lie there, oh quietest! And drink your fill -
Dream mid the mysteries of your cloud crowned hill.
Th' engulfed heights that fade in silver gloom
Your thoughts wild birthplace or their mighty tomb.

Lie down again upon your soft greenward,
And turn your eyes as usual, heavenward,
And watch the silent shadows as they fly by,
Or the warm glories of the cloudless sky.

But give us revelations of the glory -
Tell us, not grudgingly, the holy story -
Shall poets talk of inspiration lost -
Counting the trouble that the tale would cost?

I did not ask for a verse. I only said to … 'I wish someday you would give me an autograph of Tennyson' -

I wish you had been here the other night. Some people abused Wordsworth's poetry. It made me quite ill - I tried to answer their nonsense till I got quite hot - nearly cried. I have got 'Modern Painters'[19]

[19]National Gallery Archives, NGA1/22/111. Margaret to William Boxall, 24th August 1846.

A photograph of Woodlands at Aigburth, Liverpool, family home of the Sandbach family. Courtesy of Auriol, Marchioness of Linlithgow.

Ffotograff o Woodlands, Aigburth, Lerpwl, cartref y teulu Sandbach. Trwy garedigrwydd Auriol, Ardalyddes Linlithgow.

10th September 1846

My dear Mr. Boxall,
I send you as I promised the lines on Gibson's Hunter- collected - I hope improved- at any rate I have not "called the wrong names" as you and Harry have complained of!

We were so sorry to hear you had been ill- I hope now you are quite well again? You used to say fine weather made you feel well, and this is beautiful- We began to be afraid something was amiss as you even long in writing- I dreamt the night before I got your letter, such a dream- that we were out by a lake side over fine evening, gathering flowers- you were at a little distance from us- I saw you step close to the water ledge, on some bright green moss- it save way it was a dress bag, and down you went- the green moss closed up again- you were gone- what a dream- I was so glad when I awoke only to think of that stupid old boat carrying the box backwards and forwards between England and Wales! It was a wonder I did not exclaim from the mind- and remonstrate. I have had a letter from Sibson since I came here, he was just setting out to Cebano (?) near Padua for three week- I shall write to the 'Caro Autie' to meet him in Rome. If the Queen's statue is in the exhibition next year the aurora, our beautiful aurora will not be there - I am afraid it will be some time yet before she comes.

I have been drawing a spring of jasmine- copying exactly from nature- if you like it, it is for you. When we meet again and I hope that will not be more than four months hence? If so long- after Christmas, come sooner if you can. You know I was so glad to have your letter- I know you don't like writing, so I shall not expect letters from you- but always be delighted when they come- I am longing to get back in Hafodunos- I do have "pleasure in writing that word" to be in my favourite haunts again- among my flowers and my books… When will you come there again! We will not leave here before the 18th you would not think that Harry was obliged to fight with tendency to gout! And drink these odoriferous waters and bathe in sulphur! − So it is and the doctors say nothing but his active outdoors life has kept off real fits of the gout!

I have seen Bolton Abbey- and I was not disappointed- to my fancy the white door was fitting- sliding satin through the shadowy ruin. It is so beautiful- worthy of Wordsworth's poetry. I wished for you so much- I did not sketch at all ('I should have hated whatever I had done')- I could only enjoy and look silently on the beauty - the river, the woods, the stately grey ruin- But Fanwill, it is no use trying to dislike- Perhaps someday we may be there together. God bless you- my dear Mr. Boxall, ever yours, M Sandbach.

I am very happy you liked the sonnet. Thank you for accepting it so kindly. [20]

[20] National Gallery Archives, NGA1/22/112. Margaret to William Boxall, 10th September 1846.

12th October 1846

My dear Mr. Boxall,

I have just got your letter- and will answer it now- during the quietness of a wet afternoon- and before the arrival of a large pacts of friends who are coming today to spend the week with us- I am quite peeved (?) to hear of your accident- and yet it might have been so much worse that thankfully must be in the main feeling is such a case- But I shall be very anxious to hear you are well again: Such accidents are very fearful- any injury to the head must be carefully cured, and watched- do not write or exert yourself for some time, even if you feel able- Great as is the pleasure your letter gives me I could not have had you run the slightest risk- yet I hope, when you may with perfect safety, you will write and tell me so. How grateful you must have been to see your friend in haste! after the imminent days! I believe the safest thing always is to keep to the carriage or on horseback to the house. Once or twice I have been strongly tempted to spring off, or pimp out of a carriage but happily I never did- we came back here first on the 19th of September, a lovely day, and "the glorious sun" shining on Hafodunos. The flowers all so gay, and the garden lovely- the afternoon shadows lying softly on the green banks- the trees quickly tinted hence and there with autumn colours. Ah said I, I wish Mr. Boxall was here now!- When you were here the days were so wet and unlovely. A day or two after, we rode up a little way through the woods on the other side of Llanrwst I must take you there some day next summer. Then we had to leave here again for my brother's marriage, on the 6th and come back last Wednesday in wind and rain and I fear we have much wet weather in prospect. I don't know when I shall get up to the Common to take a sketch of the mountains for you it will be a showery effect!

The inscription you send me is very beautiful- and goes to one's heart. Thank you for it- I think you must have been very happy in Somersetshire. You call painting "labour"- but is it not a labour of love? It would be to me, if I painted like you. That is truth, not meant for compliment. How strange! You quote the very words "all things are busy" and which last night, and this morning which I was dressing, I was reading and thinking ones- and reading alone to Harry before breakfast- but don't say so of yourself- Remember Milton "they also serve" and he is not the less serving and glorifying God, who is silently but earnestly training up his soul in love and worship- and if opportunities are not given to us here, of making the honey and watering the flowers, we may so feed our souls on pure influences that they are made must for the work hereafter. In moments of depression one may sigh out the poet's words- but only then- I have been reading Mr. Ruskin's book- I have it now- I am very much interested in it- I cannot go along with him always, but I admire his mind, and treasure the sacredness of his feeling and the loftiness of his views- for they are very high and right- and noble. I wish you were here to talk about it- you would throw light for me perhaps on the obscene pacts- the writing here and there is most beautiful, and always full of thought, but he is involved and involves his reader sometimes in a labyrinth, where one has to go back and back to at out, and come in again an easier way. How do you find that? I would delight in knowing such a mind- when I have finished the book I will tell you how I like it all- It must be read slowly- and with attention- I could write pages about Chancer!- and our Wordsworth.

But I must have done. About the Hunter- I am extremely offended, and mean to abuse you "when I have any paper for space- which thank your stars, will be never. Honestly, I do not think the word "struggling" worked improve it- "struggling tendon stained" seems to me wrong- it is stained but not struggling, which implies action- the dog is still, but on the sketch. Am I right?- and I hope very soon when you are well.

Be careful- adieu,
M.S.
And about the other line I think you are right. And you are right to criticise.[21]

17th December 1846
Aigburth

My Dear Mr. Boxall,
I was so glad to get your letter- thought it did not bring us so good an account of your health as I hoped for, I do hope you are already better again from the change you were anticipating- and from a clearer and more bracing air. Bracing indeed- bitterly cold, perhaps I ought to say- but I walk out a good deal and enjoy the frosty weather- I wish you were here as able to enjoy it- though I have a wretched "moping" headache sometimes, which (I may say, as you do) unfits me for everything. I am sure you would not think the half hour ill spent which you bestowed on me, if you knew what pleasure your letter gave me- although I grieved to think you were still not well, I had been sadly afraid you were worse, and the sight of your handwriting was most welcome- you must be content to be but idle yet and you will get quite well. Do not grudge the time you give to your own recovery- it is absolutely necessary and a duty- I know it is painful and irksome to be obliged to be idle but sometimes pleasant thoughts glide in to comfort us, and there is a certain defence of happiness in the feeling that we are submitting as patiently as we can to a necessity that would not be laid upon us but for some good end- Don't you feel this- You made me laugh very much about the butcher- I went once to see a poor woman who had lost her husband- and she was in much grief and lamentation over his loss, I summoned up his perfections by saying with a sigh, "he was a striving man for this world" he never forgot to ask his customer "if they wanted any beef!"- I suppose it is the part of wisdom "to thrive for their world" as well as for the next- but I do believe it is a harder and more uncongenial task, which shows us, thank god that our souls are strong within us, and crave as much as our bodies do- and cannot go unfed. I have never read the Vita Miova entirely, only extracts, and notices, which always made me wish to read it and now I shall get it. When you come, which I hope will be before long, you shall see what "thoughts I have been harmonising"- not many- but if they please you I shall be very glad- unfinished yet- and too long to send in a letter. We are in the midst of Christmas holiday engagements chiefly for children, of which we have a goodly number in our family circle, and if they are going to have some Tableaux vivont next week in which we aunts and uncles are to assist- a strange medley you would think- anything but artistical!

[21]National Gallery Archives, NGA1/22/113. Margaret to William Boxall, 12th October 1846.

Great fun for the little ones- fancy an immense shoe with old mother hubbard standing with her rod, and to look like a Tableau! A sort of mock gravity on their faces, delicious to see- then we have "Moses being dressed for the fair" in which I am to be the sister Olivia, and there was great glee when they beheld me figuring in an old brocaded gown etc.- I hope you will soon write and tell us when you can come, we are obliged to go from home on the 21st January for a week- but any time except that- stay as long as you can- Take care of yourself- Harry's kindest regards- believe me ever, dear Mr. Boxall,

M.S. [22]

Hafodunos
11th June 1847

My dear Mr Boxall,
How are you all this time? Here we go on farming and rusticating and know very little of what is going with elsewhere and I am afraid we shan't see you in town this year. The Country has been most delicious - our 'broken banks' perfectly enamelled with the most charming colours - I wish you had seen them - radiant with bright wild flowers on the carpet of soft green leaves and moss - I don't know why one should wish to leave such peaceful and pleasant scenes but it is the greatest disappointment to me not to go to London this year. Especially because Gibson is coming - he was to leave Rome on the 1st of June. Ben had been so very ill but was better. You must write to us directly when you see the statue of the Queen. I want you particularly to tell me if you have seen those sculptures by the two Monti, at Colnaghi's, and if they are worthy of the praise lavished on them in the papers - one can't depend on such, in these days but I can depend on you. Will you come and see us this year and bring your drawings - not paints - you know how glad we should be anytime to see you. This note is to elicit one from you and I have nothing to tell you or say more except Harry's kind remembrances to you.

Believe me always

Yours very truly

M Sandbach

Where is Mr Ruskin now? [23]

[22]National Gallery Archives, NGA1/22/116. Margaret to William Boxall, 17th December 1846.
[23]National Gallery Archives, NGA1/22/126. Margaret to William Boxall, 11th June 1847.

28th December 1849
Woodlands

Such a cold snowy morning!

Dear Mr. Boxall,
How are you? A happy new year to you. May you have no ugly faces to look at and no green satin gowns to paint. Seriously, let us hear of you, and accept our best wishes - is there any chance of our seeing you? We want you, really, to paint that long talked picture of grey headed me before I get quite venerable. When would you like to do it? Would you come to Hafodunos as soon as the days are longer, and paint there- and then finish when I come to London in spring? I might not have time to give settings enough then- for altogether- but say what you would like- We must do it now- I mean not delay it as we have done if it is to be- and as that is decided-we had better proceed.

I have just had a letter from out Caro Autieo - he was not very well- but Ben was better. He /G/ is coming to England early in summer- Hurrah! We'll have him at your no. 5 and call him Anitico. Dear friend Gibson- there is not a purer better heart beating in this world than his. I must tell you I have a little volume of poems coming out in spring- We are here for a week or two- our cottage being lent to our sister and brother Captain and Mrs. Frans who are at home on leave- for a short time- old Mr. Sandbach is better just now. Harry is gone up to town today- but only for a day- so you won't see him- We return to Hafodunos next month. Please write to me to Aigburth and believe me dear Mr. Boxall,

Ever faithfully yours,

M Sandbach.[24]

Daeth yn wybyddus ym Mhrydain bod Margaret yn gyfaill mynwesol i Gibson ac ati hi yr ysgrifennai pobl am ei syniadau am yr artist, tra roedd hi wrthi'n paratoi ei hunangofiant. Fel cefnogwr pennaf Gibson ym Mhrydain, allai Margaret ddim peidio ag ysgrifennu at Anna Jameson(1794-1860) oedd wedi cyhoeddi erthygl ar Gibson yn yr Art Journal:

Margaret became well known in Britain as a confidante of Gibson's; people contacted her for her thoughts on the artist, whilst she worked on his biography. As Gibson champion in Britain, Margaret could not stop herself from writing to the author of an article in the Art Journal on Gibson, Anna Jameson (1794-1860):

[24]National Gallery Archives, NGA1/22/152. Margaret to William Boxall, 28th December 1849.

Hafodunos, Llanrwst,
May 15, 1849.

Madam,

I hope you will kindly excuse the liberty I am taking in writing to you. I am induced to do so from the interest with which I have just read your life of Gibson in the Art Journal. In a letter from Gibson lately received, he tells me it is yours, and very happy indeed I am to see so true and beautiful a memorial of his life thus given to the world, by one who appreciates fully both the man and his Art.

May I be permitted to mention one or two little circumstances with regard to his Works which I happen to be acquainted with, and which I am sure, from the spirit of your own work, will not be uninteresting to you.

I have also looked out a few extracts from Gibson's letter, written when the idea of the Statue of Aurora first dawned upon him — & during its progress.

We only possess two statues by Gibson — The Greek Hunter & the Aurora…

The Statue of Sappho with 'her drooping head & Lyre unstrung,' is especially interesting to us, from the circumstance that Gibson designed it with reference to the former inmate of the Library it was intended to adorn — my dear Grandfather Mr. Roscoe 'Sappho mourning for her son.'

The Angel of Hope, watching for the opening the Gates of Heaven, was originated by some lines of my father which we found after his death, & I read to Gibson when I was in Rome. The Tablet was designed in memory of him, but my Mother too died very soon after, & it is sacred to both.

We have also, besides the two Statues, a bas-relief in marble of Cupid & Psyche (flying). A cast of the Wounded Amazon, Hero & Leander & Venus & Cupid & a bust in marble. We see only too little of them, for we reside principally in Wales.[25]

I will now only add the Extracts I spoke of, & with many apologies for the length of this letter, beg you to believe me Madam,

Very truly yours,

Margaret Sandbach

P.S. In 1846 Gibson gave me some interesting accounts of conversations with you. Pray forgive me if this interest in a mutual friend has led me to write too much.[26]

Monument to Edward and Margaret Roscoe by John Gibson. Courtauld Gallery.
Cofadail i Edward a Margaret Roscoe gan John Gibson. Oriel Courtauld.

[25] They were at The Cottage, Aigburth.
[26] Mrs Stueart Erskine (Ed.), Anna Jameson letters and friendships 1812-1860, (New York, E.P. Dutton & Company, 1915), p.239-240.

Fanny Cerrito, celebrated ballerina, shown here holding a tiara with a wreath design on top of a box inscribed 'Gli Ammiratori / A Fanny Cerrito / Roma Il 22 9bre 1843'. British Museum.

Fanny Cerrito, balerina enwog, sydd yma yn gafael mewn tiara â chynllun torch arni ar ben bocs sydd â'r geiriau 'Gli Ammiratori / A Fanny Cerrito / Roma Il 22 9bre 1843'. Yr Amgueddfa Brydeinig.

Wrth i'w gyrfa fel awdur flodeuo, roedd yn rhaid iddi ymweld â Llundain yn amlach i gyfarfod â chyhoeddwyr yn ogystal â'i ffrindiau a'i hedmygwyr. Yno cafodd Margaret ei swyno gan fyd y theatr, ac yn ystod un ymweliad gwelodd berfformiadau gan Fanny Cerito, y ddawnswraig fale enwog, a Jenny Lind y gantores opera. Cafodd y ddwy eu hanfarwoli wedi hynny yn ei cherddi.

As her writing career took off, it became necessary to visit London more frequently to meet publishers as well as friends and admirers. Margaret became enthralled with the world of theatre, and it was during one of these trips she saw perform Fanny Cerrito (1817-1909), celebrated ballerina, and Jenny Lind (1820-1887) the opera singer, immortalising them later in her poetry.

Cerito as Undine, 1844

See- she comes with airy motion,
Bounding, flying, child of ocean!
Floating robes, and corall'd hair,
Arms of snowy whiteness bare;
Soft feet washed with opal water:
'Tis Undine, the Sea-King's daughter.

Now the dance she's wildly weaving;
Now she stands, her bosom heaving,
Poised and motionless, and listening,
Eye half wondering, gleaming, glistening.
Then away, to sport and hover,
O'er the captive mortal lover.

Clasp him close, Undine, Undine!
It shall not be, as it hath been;
Though the earthly spell is strong,
It shall fail and break ere long;
And the new found love shall flee,
When the ocean maid shall be
Bound to Earth in fatal union,
Sweet though now the strange communion.

Wandering through their sparry caves
Roofed with changing beryl waves,
Sea-nymphs mourn the lost Undine
Amid her bowers no longer seen.
  They wail and weep
  And from the deep
    They call her home,
    "Undine! oh come!"
  They leave their purple beds
    Of sea-weed rare,
  And bow their shell-crowned heads
    And bind their flowing hair;
    "Where hast thou fled, Undine,
    Our dear delight?
  Is thy young beauty seen,
    By mortal sight?
  Seek not the land,
    Here is thy peace,
  Pure as these glassy streams
    That never cease.

"Come to the sea-green bower,
  Adorned for thee
With gem and glittering oar,
  And fairy tree.
The music-breathing shell
  All silent lies;
Till thou awake and swell
  Its harmonies.
Here is the coral crown
  Thy hair to deck;
And soft pearls once thine own,
  To wreathe thy neck;
And here the azure dress
  Dyed in the wave,
Who for thy loveliness
  His colours gave.
Oh come, Undine, we mourn,
And fill thy crystal urn
  With our fast-falling tears,-
  And ocean murmuring, hears,
          And calls thee home;
          Come then, oh come!"

Vainly they call. Look where she stands, amazed;
In startled action, with her white arms raised,
And eyes fixed on a phantom shape that falls
Beside her, as she treads those earthly halls!
To mortal lover given, the sea-born maid
Bears with her now a mortal body's shade;
Faithless, ah faithless to her purer birth,
Her spirit form is now a thing of Earth.

    She knows it not, she darts away-
    It haunts, it tracks her fearful way-
    She bounds, she flies, in wild despair,
    But still she sees the shadow there.
    It takes her form, it mocks her grace,
    It hunts her steps in equal chase.
    And now her fear is all surprise-
    She pauses, turns, nor longer flies;
    Then upward with elastic bound
    She springs, and leaves it on the ground.
    One moment only- child of ocean,
    Lost in maze of airy motion,-
    The shadow still must follow thee;
    Till the mortal spell is broken,
      Till the last farewell is said,
    Till the welcome home is spoken,
      And the sea-nymphs crown thy head.[27]

[27]Margaret Sandbach, 'Cerito as Undine', Aurora and other poems, (London: Pickering, 1850), p.90-3.

VI

The Weary Muse, pasted by Margaret onto the front page of her 1851 diary.
Courtesy of Auriol, Marchioness of Linlithgow.

The Weary Muse, a bastiwyd gan Margaret ar dudalen flaen ei dyddiadur am 1851.
Trwy garedigrwydd Auriol, Ardalyddes Linlithgow.

'...as the distance lengthens between us I feel that our souls draw closer together...'[1]

Erbyn 1851 roedd Margaret wedi blino'n llwyr ac yn gyson glaf. Mae ei dau ddyddiadur sydd wedi goroesi yn gyfrolau A5 sydd wedi'u rhwymo mewn lledr â dalennau clawr marmor cain o waith llaw. Mae dyddiaduron 1851 (clawr gwyrdd) a 1852 (clawr du), yn sôn am ei misoedd prin o iechyd da, y diagnosis o ganser y fron, a'i threfniadau am y materion corfforol ac ysbrydol yn barod ar gyfer ei marwolaeth. Mae darllen ei meddyliau wrth iddi ystyried ei ffawd yn rhoi golwg deimladwy ar feddwl dynes a wyddai fod ei marwolaeth gerllaw ac na allai dim ei rwystro.

Prif ddigwyddiad cymdeithasol y flwyddyn honno oedd yr Arddangosfa Fawr yn y Palas Grisial. Roedd hon yn ddathliad o hyder a chyrhaeddiad yr Ymerodraeth Brydeinig. Bu disgwyl mawr amdani a daeth yr ymwelwyr o bell ac agos. Teithiodd John Gibson draw i weld ei waith yno. Ond wrth i seren Gibson gyrraedd ei brig, pylu oedd goleuni Margaret.

Yn ei llythyr olaf at y Fonesig Smith, cyfaddefodd Margaret ei bod hi'n clafychu:

> *Hafodunos*
> *April 21st 1851*
>
> *'...I am frightened of the heat & bustle & fatigue of this great Exhibition - never being very strong & just now, from repeated attacks of colds & coughs, more inclined than usual to be quick...'[2]*

Doedd Margaret byth i gyfarfod y cefnogwr brwd o'i gwaith.

By 1851, Margaret was exhausted and frequently ill. Her two surviving diaries are both leather bound, A5 journals with exquisite hand-marbled endpapers. 1851 has green cover and 1852 a black cover, they record her last few months of fleeting good health, diagnosis with breast cancer, and the arranging of affairs, both spiritual and corporeal, in preparation for death. Her outpourings try to reason with her lot and are incredibly touching glimpses into the mind of a woman who knew that death was near and she was unable to stop its march.

The great social event of the year was the Great Exhibition at Crystal Palace, a great celebration of British Imperial confidence and achievement. Much anticipated, it drew visitors from far and wide, including John Gibson, who travelled to see his work displayed.

In her final letter to Lady Smith, Margaret admitted her weakening state:

Margaret was never to meet this important champion of her work.

[1]Aberystwyth, National Library of Wales, MS 20566E-126. John Gibson to Margaret, September 27th 1851.

'The night is far spent, the day is at hand. Let us therefore cast off the works of darkness and put upon us the armour of light'[3]

May it please God to bless me and all who are dear to me, in this New Year – to grant us knowledge of his life, and his truth, as our greatest comfort – and give us strength to perform what he requires of us. May our eyes be directed to that beacon – lights shining above, which can guide us over the darkest and roughest paths of Earth.

Wednesday January 1st
Fine morning, and mild coming in of the New Year. Harry went hunting in Cheshire – and I had rather a quieter morning than usual. Wrote a while at story – and drew a little. Went out to buy stuff to rigg myself out as 'the Welsh woman' and appeared in s.d costume at Henry Harrisons at night. Very bad headache all day – Henry tired – gay evening – and children in… glee.

January Saturday 4 January
Morning drew, afternoon went to Liverpool and bought all my things for the 'tree' for my party on the 8th. Met Harry returning from hunting and he came home with me and we had our tea and 'a chop', very snug.

Wednesday 8th Went to town at 11. Shopped. Took Aunt R [Roscoe] – bought goodies for evening and my party came and went, and all did well – except dear Harry having a headache, and declaring such parties 'a nuisance!' – about 50 – chiefly children - Glad to get it over – but enjoyed seeing the children. Thursday, 9th Drew a great deal went to Woodlands in the afternoon Harry and Willie hunted and came home to late dinner

Friday 10 January
Watched Mr. P [Pidgeon] finish my favourite and beloved mountain view from the Common. This evening we drank tea at Mr Jevons to meet Mr and Mrs Hornblower – Sandbach and Alfred and Jenny Dixon dined with us first. Pleasant evening at

Mr Jevons' – was introduced to James Thornley who is to marry Laura and was much pleased with him.

Saturday 11 January
Morning drew – Jenny Dixon came – then Mr Appleton and 2 little girls, then Julia – then Mr Alex. Smith after luncheon Harry and I and Sandbach Parker rode to Cunninghams. Nursery gardens and to Thirlwall. I rode Julia, Horse 'Lancer' a very nice one. Evening spent at Woodlands and poor old Father in his bed as usual, said "Come as often as you can in the Evenings, and sit a bit with me".

Tuesday 14 January
Drawing lesson – drew Betws-y-Coed. Dined yesterday at Woodlands to meet Gilbert - who is come for a few days. Callers in after today and got very little done.

Wednesday 15 January
Intended writing to Gibson but wrote one or two notes first & then Emma Martin came & staid to luncheon & in the afternoon I rode to Ambroses on Julia's horse & dined at the Zwilcheubach's so another idle day & bad headache to boot

Thursday 16 January
Wrote to Gibson. After went to town, Anne went with me. Shopped, saw Fanny and the dear children in Rodney St. At house this evening.

Friday 17 January
Drawing Lesson. So pleasant Effie and Elizabeth Hanmer came. Dined at home – no one else.

Sunday 19th January
We drank tea at Woodlands today. Yesterday we took them to town. Saw St Georges Hall and had a small party to discuss one of the celebrations of Lord Mostyn's Grandson coming of age. He is a pleasing young man apparently.

Have read a very sweet little book called 'Maiden and married like of Mary Powell afterwards Mistress Milton' – by (Lady Willoughby) Mrs Rathebone written in a beautiful spirit, also cleverly, and with much animation – There are some exquisite touches of feeling – tis also full of nature. Simplicity and pathos – It keeps pretty close to the second text - of Miltons early life with his first wife –

Monday 20 January
Morning drew and prepared picture for Mr Laurence. At 12 went to Liverpool with Miss Howells by Railway. Afterwards travelled with Fanny. Dear little Eddie winds himself round my head – sweet gentle darling! Harry went to Ruthin. Evening at home. He returned before 7. Very strong and wet.

Tuesday 21 January
Drawing lesson, Mr Pidgeon tells me he has an appointment in London & will go there. Very sorry he leaves L'pool but glad for his sake. Afterwards went to Woodlands…

[3]Romans 13:12

Henry Harrison (1795-1871) was another successful Liverpool merchant whose marriage to Mary Rosina Sandbach in 1835 united two entrepreneurial families. Private Collection.

Henry Harrison (1795-1871), masnachwr llwyddiannus arall o Lerpwl. Unwyd dau deulu entrepreneuraidd pan briododd Mary Rosina Sandbach ym 1835. Casgliad Preifat.

Wednesday 22 January
Left at 11 ¼ for Coed Coch. Arrived there soon after 4. Late party in the house.

Thursday 23 January
Day fine. Walked out in the afternoon and drew in the morning. Country beautiful.

24 Friday January
Ball at Abergele at night and William [Sandbach] came to dinner.

Sunday 26th January
Thinking over the past week, it looks to me very worldly and unblessed. Yet there were kind and good friends where I have been. But we were accepted with worldly things and thoughts. I see too much so – and seeing others so makes me sad – so I trust I am aware of the dangers. Self-indulgence, luxury and their train of weakening influences will soon make us unfit for the strict, self-denying life of duty. Oh let us not fall into so great a snare but exert ourselves to look actively for the soul, rather than for the body… Keep our hearts fixed on the great realities of Eternity, remembering that this life is passing – swiftly passing – and leaves us only those things to keep, which are eternal – nothing is eternal which is not holy – oh then letters purify over affections – our hope – our duty, even – making all spiritual –

Saturday 25 January
Everybody late after the revels – but I was not sleepy nor tired much – we walked out before lunch – and left for home directly after – and reached to late dinner – William with us.

Monday 3rd February
Last drawing lesson, very sorry.

Wednesday 5th February
Drew. Went to town Mrs. Parker with me – called on Cath and Mrs. Savage – Mrs. Bald etc. Harry hunted – and we dined late.

Thursday 6th February
Drew – view of mountains for my cousins. Bachelors ball all night. H. not well with threatening of influenza. Cured by abstinence. Ball pretty and gay.

Friday 7th February
Finished drawing. William Caldwell Roscoe dined and we all went to Mrs. Butlers reading of Henry VIII at night. We agreed she read well – but exaggerated parts, and wanted refinement, and discrimination of the delicate parts. What a magnificent play! – She deserved the gratitude of the public for bringing these works so well before them – for, after all, even with her faults, it is a fine thing to hear her read them – and who would do it better? Or as well?

…This week the Heatons were to have spent with us – but are prevented by a death in their family Miss Ll. Williams – Got a little Skye terrier for stables and christened him "Dandy" after the good old dog.

Saturday 8 February
Got to my writing again for this morning – till interrupted by callers at 12.30 PM went over the M.S connected and added in parts.

Sunday 9th February
Bad cold in my head – very bad – in doors.

Monday 10th February
Morning wrote. Afternoon rode with Willie to Edge Lane. They were out. My cold still bad tho' better…

Tuesday 11th February
Dinner party at house.

Wednesday February 12th
Went to Liverpool lunched with Fanny and brought her back in the Brougham to make calls at the Aigburth. Dined at John Tinne's.

Thursday February 13th
Wellington Ball I went for certain persons – though not well. Mounted my new drawings which I did with Mr Pidgeon. Ellen Mason sang sweetly and Miss Haywood also, very well, grand voice. Very fine intelligent girl. Dear Ellen Mason so pleasant – Finished 'Villa Verocchio – on youth of Leonardo da Vinci' pretty little book, but rather poor to what I expected – laboured writing.

Saturday 15th February
Poorly with sore throat and feverish cold. Got I don't know how. In home all day. Wrote letter and got on with writing. Copied, and also wrote 13 new pages. Harry and William went hunting Sunday. Again, obliged to stay in, throat very sore and limbs weak. Day exquisite, as yesterday and day before, Violets, anemones etc plenty.

Monday 16th February
Morning wrote a story. After went to Woodlands to help in wedding preparations addressing cards etc. Staid there till 5 ½. Very poorly with cold but wrapt up well.

Tuesday 17th February
Got up, very poorly after a bad night. Throat, head all ill. Have been much perplexed in thought and very anxious lately on a certain subject connected with a person dear to me. I feel that I ought not to allow undue anxiety to press upon me especially remembering that all is in God's hands. This will is best. Whichever way this turns out, may I so look upon it, and if disappointment comes, let me not whine, but help to clean and soothe which must suffer more than mine. So much more yet I may God grant a good issue to this hope. Bless and prosper and fulfil it. Oh how much we hope when a strong affection urges us towards it!

A horse prancing by John Gibson, given as a gift to Margaret by Gibson, sepia wash on paper. Private Collection.

A horse prancing gan John Gibson, a roddwyd yn anrheg i Margaret gan Gibson, golch sepia ar bapur. Casgliad Preifat.

Jane Hornblower (1797-1853). She was the second daughter of William Roscoe and like many of the Roscoe family she was a poet. Her first volume, Poems by one of the Authors of Poems for Youth by a Family Circle was published in 1820, and her second, Poems, in 1843. Private Collection.

Jane Hornblower (1797-1853). Hi oedd ail ferch William Roscoe ac fel nifer o'r teulu hwnnw roedd hi'n barddoni. Cyhoeddwyd ei chyfrol gyntaf, Poems by one of the Authors of Poems for Youth by a Family Circle ym 1820, a'i hail gyfrol Poems ym 1843. Casgliad Preifat.

Went in the Brougham to Dr Drysdale who gave me some medicine. Felt better in after but too poorly all day to do anything but read a bit…Have got youth of 'Leonardo da Vinci' which disappoints me - a dry little book though the subject is very interesting.

Wednesday 18th February
Better – but still appeared foolishly went to dinner to Mr. J Molyment and felt worse all the time I was there. Today Mr and Miss Rathbone called. Miss Haywood and Miss Myers etc.

Thursday 19th February
Had a dreadfully bad night - fever - restlessness oppression. Dearest Harry so kind - got hardly any sleep. I stayed in bed till noon and felt a little better. Mr and Mrs Parker dined. Went to bed rather better this time.

Friday 21 February
…felt very weak, but fever gone, then wrote a little, also to Gibson but being feeble I did not do much and slept now and then…

The founders of the Historic Society of Lancashire and Cheshire featuring Margaret's art tutor, Henry Clarke Pidgeon (in the centre). National Portrait Gallery.

Sefydlwyr Cymdeithas Hanes Swyddi Caerhirfryn a Chaer, sy'n cynnwys Henry Clarke Pidgeon (yn y canol), tiwtor celf Margaret. Oriel Genedlaethol y Portreadau.

Saturday 23rd February

Took out the Portfolio of my beloved Mother's letters. I read over some. Most touching and beautiful, I never can read them without being deeply moved – sorrowfully, though thankfully. Such a pious soul. So grateful, so loving, so bound to duty. Oh dearest Mother, thou art now in peace and joy. Thy spirit made meet for eternal life and happiness is now in its congenial home. Oh may thy blessed example be ever with me to suspect me in the path of sight and to preserve me from Evil, from worldliness, from deepness, from doubt. From vain confidence. Keep me humble – aspiring- gentle – yet firm true and sincere. As thou went! Ah, all thy dear influence did not die, when that drooping eye closed for ever. That voice was not lost when the parched fixed lips, refused to utter the last – last pronounced words!!

In the house with exception of a turn out in the sunshine. Fine and clear. But East wind.

Monday 24th February

Morning went to Woodlands got fresh flowers and prepared for an arrival of friends. At 1.30 Lady Erskine and Miss Erskine came. After lunch we went to Mrs Lawnwell. She was very well and kind and they were delighted. Evening a party of ten to dinner.

Tueday 25th February

Morning shopping in Liverpool. Afternoon Sir Watkin Wynne arrived. Evening Welsh ball at which 940 people attended and it went off with great spirits.

Wednesday 26th February

Morning examining of school children at Welsh school, very interesting. Then to St. George's Hall. … Evening dinner party here 14.

Thursday 27th February

Lady Erskine left at two. I went to Woodlands and was busy arranging flowers for the wedding tomorrow…

(Diary includes an extended printed letter in 9pt description of a wedding in Liverpool, by Margaret Sandbach. Written at The Cottage, March 1st 1851)

Sunday March 17th

Mr Hesketh preached a more interesting sermon than usual this morning. We dined early and then went to town, taking Alan Mason home. Harry and I went to Renshaw St after service and to dear Mother's Grave. The sun shone on the churchyard which tho dull and town-like is quiet and restive and it looked more cheerful than usual. - 'Oh how I should like to see her dear face again' I sighed. 'You will see it again in Heaven, Love' said my kind Harry and I wiped away my few tears and went away cheerful in that thought. - As we walked home, we heard the peals of the organ in the 'Church of the Apostles' in Canning St. We stopped at the door to listen and were told we might come in - we went in - it was beautiful. They sang the Virgins song 'My soul doth magnify the Lord' and gave the simplest blessing - and now I know the inside of the curious building which looked like a broken promise, standing unfinished, yet inviting, which I have wondered about so long - the people occupy the lower end of the chancel, sitting on chairs, common wooden chairs, with little cushions for kneeling.

Monday 18th March

…Began a drawing to help raffle for Mr Harrisons' pictures…

Wednesday 20th March

Harry went to Plas Heaton.

Sunday 23rd March

Stanley Place. Am much troubled by the deadness of my heart, the coldness of my faith, the poverty of my prayers, the utter worldliness of my feelings and yet all the time knowing am dreading my state. Am also much shocked by the announcement of Miss Martineau's infidel views (so it is said) In her I behold the consequence of the dreadful pride of human reason. It's abused *power. Good Lord! Deliverers from ourselves from our doubts, from our weakness, pride and from the influence and operation of all Evil…*

Tuesday 25th March
Morning wrote to Harry to Denby (sic) to tell him of Joseph's death. I shall now go to him at Hafod as soon as I can…Got home in good time and finished correction of large drawing which I had sent for from
Liverpool, reframed and hung it up…

Wednesday 6th March
Letter from dearest Harry, I go tomorrow to join him…Little Dandy came in a basket. I never saw such a sharp, jolly dog. All our other things arrived and we begun to get settled as soon as we could. The school I find in good order and it has been a very healthy Winter for the children. Which is surprising considering it has been unusually damp and wet.

March 28th March
Breakfast at Woodlands. Bid goodbye to the kind parents and all the rest and left for Hafodunos at 11…Had a good journey, (dear Wille took me across the water and reached Haf at 5.30) Harry meeting me in village. I came in a carriage and servants in another- the old bridge is down and the new one begun - such a chasm it makes. So glad to get to Haf, oh peace! oh rest!

Hafodunos

29th March
Went all about the garden and afterwards to school and pleased with everything. Plants never looked so well in the gardens and in good order. Guthrie [the gardener] has done wonders – the bulbs he planted in the West Wall are beautiful. bad cough. Wet day. Cough bad not out. Arranged many things in house. Jane came up and settled. Heywood arrived with the horses. Finished up a flower drawing and packed another to send to S. Yates for the Harrison raffle.

Sunday
Peaceful and blessed. Felt approaching the dawn of returning faith and love which has of late in cold within me. And thankful and would be patient.

Monday – Tuesday – Wednesday
Thursday – Friday – Saturday
Quiet happy days - the only difference being that the beginning of the week I was ill with my bad cough. By Thursday got out fine weather but East Wind.

Friday
Morning - had a slight attack in my head but with care & quiet & not writing at my story it went off. Passed nearly all day in open air - dreadful headache after the numbness went off. Went to see poor Jane Hughes nearly dying, To Coed Coch on horseback but coughed much afterwards. Mrs Wynne's Spring plants are very pretty. Nice hour in the garden.

April 5th
Cut down many of the large Camellias. Frost last night. We have not seen a creature this week and have been very happy by ourselves… Have got on this week with story.

Monday 7th April
I went out a little though not yesterday on account of my cold and cough.

Tuesday 8th April
At school today…

April Saturday 19th
Have spent the week in Liverpool. Stayed at Woodlands - as my cough was too bad to venture out at night. Our dear Mother most kind. Poor Father very suffering and worse on the whole. Sad to see him suffer and we can do nothing to keep him…

Julia Sandbach (1827-1890) was the youngest child of Samuel and Elizabeth Sandbach.
Private Collection.

Julia Sandbach (1827-1890) oedd plentyn ieuengaf Samuel and Elizabeth Sandbach.
Casgliad Preifat.

Anne Parker (1803-1890) was the eldest child of Samuel and Elizabeth Sandbach. She married her second cousin, Charles Stewart Parker, a Liverpool merchant in 1826. Private Collection.

Anne Parker (1803-1890) oedd plentyn hynaf Samuel and Elizabeth Sandbach. Priododd ei chyfyrder, Charles Stewart Parker, masnachwr yn Lerpwl ym 1826. Casgliad Preifat.

Left Woodlands this morning, rather suffering still, with cold and cough which prevented my going out yesterday… Drove over new bridge for the first time on arriving at Hafodunos - church rather better attended. Sacrament administered to about 20 people.

April 21 Monday
Looked at story. Gardened. Cough and cold better today.

Tuesday 22 April
Very sad account of poor Mr. Sandbach's sufferings…

25th April
Friday Morning
Lewis arrived from Woodlands at 5.30 with a summons to our poor suffering father. Greatly alarmed Harry started off instantly on horseback at 10. I followed and arrived at 2. Found him very ill. Greatly exhausted and in much pain. So thankful we have got here. Gilbert arrived today about 9pm (26th) All night sufferings dreadful but some with lasting patience! Spasms at times… About 11, poor dear Mother laid down beside him where she had lain for near 50 years. We were up and down all night and oh how I grieved to hear those sad moans. I was lastly in bed with Harry for two hours at the beginning of the night. Thinking it might last longer. But Harry never left him after morn. Till he went to wash himself at half past 6 when he was suddenly called back. We assembled around him and saw him expire in peace at quarter to 7.

Death of our good father 26th April 1851 at a quarter before 7 o'clock - a Saturday. I believe 'Henry' was the last name on his lips. I thought he wanted to say something to him. Articulation for the last hour or two was very difficult. But the mind and perceptions were all clear and the physical vigour (shown by moving himself, drawing on his night cap, shortly before he breathed his last) was unimpaired saved by the local disease which was long warring out the powers of endurance. His martyr like patience and his trust in God are great lessons which I think we never shall forget. For the last ten minutes all was peace and serenity.

May 6th
I have not kept my journal carefully which I now regret. But the past week ending in funeral which took place on Saturday 3rd May. Has been one of much trial to me. Besides the event which deprives the dear family around me of a parent of myself of a most kind and affectionate friend. I have again had a warning of the uncertainty of my own life and have looked on this sweet spring and the bursting beauty of nature of perhaps the last that may be granted me on earth. I have been greatly tired and troubled in spirit and made great exertions to keep up. But hope still now and then glides in and now I humbly seek better consolations… Had a very interesting hour perusing a sketch of Mr. Sandbach's life, written by himself for the Mother and children. It is very characteristic and excellent shows a very upright, clear mind and vigorous powers. Great piety and humility, warm affections. A most valuable and useful heirloom as well as being as otherwise precious to his children. For such wise counsel as his worldly career enabled him to give must be useful to all.

7th May
…feel a little better today, not so tired and very thankful and yet afraid that feeling better may make me less mindful of my state, at the least, what is our state? Mortal – fleeting – even as this flower soon withered – keep alive in our hearts a conviction a coming certainty of death and things eternal.

May 10th
… felt low about myself, struggled to keep up and was not unhappy…

Monday 12th May
Morning wrote at story. Afternoon went riding with dearest Harry to the new cottages Rhos-y-Mawr. Came home all along the new road from the common. Oh how I enjoyed it! How precious these hours are, now I believe them to be numbered and few! How lovely the mountains. How sweet all nature. How beautiful Hafodunos in its present and promising state. How wide, how wide and rich a

field for continued usefulness and congenial occupation. How I loved it, how above all I loved my Harry, my dearest, dearest one. And longed for his future happiness now and forever. It was hard to realise the conviction that I must leave him so soon and forever, oh my God, strengthen me in this for I am weak…

May 13th
A delicious, bright Spring day. All nature lovely. Harry and I and Guthrie planted out many things and thinned the green house. It was like older times so sweet and dear…

Wednesday 14th May
…Decided to go to London to consult Dr about me. We are to start tomorrow. My body feels like it used before I took a cold plunge in bathing - my mind anxious to bear up and be cheerful. I dread the worst and therefore hope my shock any certainty may not overpower me.

Gathered Monday evg May 12th by the side of the walk between the steps & the waterfall. - Drying flowers reminds me of Early Days when Mr Pennant at Downing taught me the proper way of doing them - to put small bits of blotting paper between any parts that touch, even between the stamen & petals of a flower - lay them first on a sheet of the blotting paper - change it as they dry. I used to do groups of garden flowers & they looked like painted flowers. Mr P(ennant) showed me some done by Lady Caroline years before which were beautiful.

Friday 16 May
…at 2 Mr Hodgson came. Very kind to me. Very candid - has bad opinion of my case - a tumour in my breast. Proposes to bring Brodie tomorrow. I was prepared for this in some degree. Still so decided an opinion is a shock at first to me and to my dearest and kindest Harry. We wrote some letters before Post time and then talked quietly over things - cried a little, prayed much in our hearts and endeavour to trust in God and & be calm. Bad headache and noise in the street so great - I could not sleep much.

Saturday 17th May
Morning to new water colours. Some lovely things especially Bennett, Penley and Hague. He spent near an hour and a half pleasantly not forgetting my troubles but yet enabled to feel pleasure as evolved in the sweet drawings. So many of Wales!

…at 3.30 Sir Benjamin Brodie and Mr Hodgson came. The former like Gibson in face - Kind and attentive in manner - examined my case. Advises us to wait a month, if no change takes place and come up again. They don't recommend an operation - ordered some medicine. This is a small reprieve. I may get some, even much, of my worldly affairs in order and be ready to leave them. I may school my mind and affection further, and wean myself from my beloved one as far as I can - and from my sweet home. Oh my best my beloved Harry - my rock and support next to my God, how I bless and love you! God reward you my darling.

Sunday 18th May
…It is curious that now I seem to look to the past on earth – my thoughts scarcely can look forward. My favourite guessings and wonderings and hopes are all gone. I only think of what has been.

Monday 19th May
Left London by express at 9 - reached Rhyl before 4 & at Hafodunos before 7pm.

Wednesday 21st May
…Afternoon at schools [Llangernyw] where I was unable to go on as usual teaching and feeling quite cheerful and glad to be at work again. After school [I] lingered in the village and took a sketch of the church, wishing to do it for Harry but felt rather tired and gave up soon.

Friday 23rd May
…I rode to Coed Coch on Princess and Harry on Prince. It did not hurt me and I was very thoughtful for the grateful and refreshing exercise…

Charles Stewart Parker (1800-1868), one of Henry and Margaret's closest friends. He and his wife helped to nurse Margaret during her illness, and Charles was at Hafodunos to support Henry during her final days. Private Collection.

Charles Stewart Parker (1800-1868), un o gyfeillion mynwesol Henry a Margaret. Bu ef a'i wraig yn helpu i ofalu am Margaret yn ystod ei gwaeledd, ac roedd Charles yn Hafodunos er mwyn bod yn gefn i Henry yn ystod ei ddyddiau olaf. Casgliad Preifat.

A white spider lily by Margaret. Private Collection.

Lili wen gan Margaret. Casgliad Preifat.

Opposite: Margaret's painting skills improved in both composition and quality under the supervision of Mr. Pidgeon. This beach scene was painted on the shores of the Conwy Estuary. Private Collection.

Gyferbyn: Gwellodd sgiliau peintio Margaret o ran cyfansoddiad ac ansawdd dan gyfarwyddyd Mr. Pidgeon. Peintiwyd yr olygfa hon o draeth ar aber yr afon Conwy. Casgliad Preifat.

June 1st

May 31st has been more lovely than I could describe. The dingle so gay with wild flowers and also full of light and beauty. I walked round the churchyard and found all the ivy planted on the church last November doing well - Very glad. I looked at my last resting place, a bank facing the East and looking to the Hills. A very calm pleasant place to lie in, I thought. Oh if I could by faith as by sight thee dwelling place of my soul.

June 3 Wednesday

…To Pandy school. 75 children on books, 65 in school. John Price earnest in teaching but himself untaught. School undisciplined but lively and active and capable of doing some good. Harry thought it was doing some good. Then to Cefn Ffynnon. Paid David £1. Poor David. Perhaps I shall never see him again. Took a long and earnest look at him and at his little house to which we made so many a pleasant excursions, shook hands and said 'Farewell. The mountains looked splendid, the glorious mountains. Drove home through Pandy and over the common. Heywood rode Prince and I often turned round to look at his bounding step and arching neck and think how often he had carried me over these roads so free and glad…

Friday 6th June

Left dear Haf at 8.20am. Took a walk in the garden, gathered some flowers to take with me - felt happy but so sad! Could hardly keep in my sob, as I took my last look and it was so beautiful.-Reached Liverpool at 1 1/4 - Being here [Woodlands] among so much life and kindness would I fear make me sometimes forget my state and coming sufferings and I might grow weak in grace and strength.

June 15 Monday

…started for London at 1/4 p11 - rooms at Almonds.

Tuesday 17th

…saw Mr Hodgson. He decided a meeting with Brodie tomorrow. After he was gone we took a drive and saw the Crystal Palace outside and met the Queen in Hyde Park. Willie dined with us. This morning Gibson came to see me having arrived on Saturday. So kind and true.

Wednesday 18th June

Morning to Crystal Palace with Willie and Gibson. Panizzi was there and others with Gibson on the Fine Arts Committee - judging - Afternoon Brodie & Hodgson - the report has cheered us 'No Worse' Oh I am going home again for another month, with my dear Harry!!

Thursday 19th June

…Morning to Royal Academy Exhibition. I liked the R.A. Gibson met us…

Friday 20th June

…Left London…A blind Lady all alone in our carriage interested me much. Blind – lovely – delicate – poor soul! She told me she lost her sight 'partly through trouble'. How I wished I could do something for her… Reached Haf before tea…

Wednesday 25th June

…I walked to Cefn-isa to see sick boy also made my calls on the sick…

June 26th

Felt well today and did so enjoy my walk with Harry. Oh thank God for these days yet spared to me. May I use them as I ought. And may he bless us both.

Friday 27th June

Very hot day…we did not go out except in the evening a little. Carting hay to stack yard to Caerllo reminded me of old days in hay fields. How pleasant!

Saturday 28th June

Left for Liverpool at 1 ½ and reached Woodlands about 7 soon after.

Gilbert Sandbach (1817-1882). Henry's younger brother, Gilbert married Margaret Maxwell and had 10 children. Their children were treasured by Margaret and Henry. Private Collection.

Gilbert Sandbach (1817-1882). Priododd Gilbert, brawd iau Henry, â Margaret Maxwell a chawsant 10 o blant. Roedd eu plant yn gannwyll llygaid Margaret a Henry. Casgliad Preifat.

June 1851

I hope I may address you this though I don't know you well, except by your character and your works, which have often made me long to know you personally better.

But this wish will now probably never be fulfilled on earth. I have just been reading your sermon 'The Shadow of Death'. I am now, myself standing within that shadow; which is deepening over me day by day. Not as it is deepening to the eyes of all men as a coming certainty. To me it is present and visible, it enfolds me. 'I die daily'

My experience accords truly to a great deal you say in that sermon but not to all. When it pleases God to tell you, that you must die, that Death is at hand, even at the door. I think, that you your heart, life will seem a thing to be loved less, and heaven appear to you brighter and happier than life even did. I say this very fervently, I hope very sincerely, - but if, I, so far inferior to you in all things — can in these moments so far realise the unseen with an undetermined eye, on it faint but beautiful dawning — how you not regard it! Earthly love sweet affections, are still as dear and precious, and we rest in them as fondly — but they do not lure us to stay — nature is still as lovely and as cherishing but instead of saying alas! You leave me, she says, behold my beauty; but a faint image of that which you are ever to behold.

I have had a beautiful and peaceful home, surrounded by love and all that want could desire of grace and sweetness, but I do not feel it so great a pang to go. In reading your sermon I have had a feeling but not a strong one, that I have not sufficiently realised my state, or I should feel it more sad. But then I dismissed this feeling, knowing it was one you never meant to arouse — and turned to the hope that by God's blessed help I had been enabled, so as to 'cast my blessed remembrances' and 'aspirations' and 'dear images' into my 'conception of things unseen' that I am less 'held back by the present. Oh true, true, true…

It is, as you say, in humble faith, above we meet our end — no transport, no joy, save the glad thankfulness that we are upheld. But this is a glad thankfulness. It makes us sing unto the Lord a new song. It is what we never felt before and what (I venture to believe) now fully experience but those who are made aware that death is very near to them.

I thank you for your beautiful and heart-instructing sermon and I pray God to bless you for the comfort you have given to many, and to spare you to do his will further on Earth.

Margaret Sandbach[4]

[4]Copy made 23rd June 1852. Henry found this letter amongst Margaret's papers and sent it onto Martineau shortly after her death. Why did Margaret not send this letter?

100

August 4th

…Reached home today after an absence of 3 weeks - we left for London on Monday 14th July - staid there until Wednesday 30th - finished Mrs Lawrence's drawing of Edinburgh - poorly these few days…

August 10th

Looking over what is previously written here I am finding all this space left for continued record of thought, I feel as though the suspension of immediate danger in regard to my health has brought it some slackness in the endeavour to prepare myself for it… Turned by the lightest wind of hope, blown over from our purposes, attracted by earthly cares and earthly pleasures. And yet, it was almost with regret I found I was till (as far as medical skill could be) destined for a little longer life… I expressed this in the papers which in the form of letters I have written to my dear Harry for his comfort here after. I need not repeat here what were my feelings. But I desire in every place to express my deep and yet too faint gratitude to my gracious Father for this longer space to grant me. I cannot rejoice and be glad in this new breath of life and hope, to look forward to a little time yet in my dear home with my dear husband. To see for a little longer my friends that are dear and hear their words of kindness and affection.

Today, Sunday 12th August, I went to church in the morning and in the afternoon remained at home. Having not been well for a few days I was listless and heavy and could not rouse my mind to active thought or devotional fervour. May I never cease to struggle with bodily infirmities and influences, today I yielded too much. Weariness and weaknesses got the better of me…

Sometimes I fear that I rely too confidently on the mercy and tenderness of my heavenly Father. And that I do not feel that dread and remorse on account of my sinfulness which I ought.

How much it lessens our mere fear and revulsion of feeling at the idea of death when we look upon it as a circumstance of our being… Alike to all and that in it merely lay down this outward case which is now the instrument by which the mind works, just as we should lay down a tool or implement when called. When called on to pause, by master or friend for whom we were working… I used to have a horror of the externals of death – a mysterious dread of its powers and ideas about burial, painful and doubtless mistaken. The day of my Mother's death was less trying to me than the day of her burial. And I still think their rites are often too hastily performed and much unsettled in that instance. But I can feel now that my soul is so truly independent of my body that I can look upon the decay of the mortal part without pain. As if I were from a far conscious that the outer rags of the earthly garments were laid aside and were mingling with the dust. Nothing more to me than this hand by which I write would be if cut off and thrown away…

Wednesday 13th August

…Gibson and Boxall arrived before we got home - very pleasant evening…

Thursday 14th August

…Mr Boxall helped me with my rose and drew a bit for me…

Friday 15th August

…I sat to Mr Boxall…

Tuesday 19th August

…Morning sat - picture getting on…

Wed 20th August

…Gibson and I have begun to write to me memoranda of his early life - he dictating it and writing. It is very interesting…

Friday 22nd August

…Harry sat to Mr Boxall and I got some writing done with G. - most evenings we read Wordsworth, Hood, Coleridge, Campbell, Tennyson - so pleasant…

Saturday 23rd August

…Poor dear Gibson rec'd news of Mr Ben's death. Harry broke it to him gently. We are so sorry. Evg on the mountain & Llanrwst saddened for Gibson - but so lovely!!…

Monday 25th August –

…Boxall left…

Saturday Sept 6th

Evening. Am sorry to have neglected my journal lately, partly having been more unwell than usual & suffering a good deal of pain & also having friends with me who occupy my time & thoughts. Gibson and I have gone on each morning writing down some memorial of his works, or opinion on art, or his life. We have generally dined early and gone to the mountain with Mr Pidgeon in the evenings and enjoyed the glorious view fully. He (Pidgeon) has made a fine sketch of the Snowdon range etc from the Abbey road just below the road to Llanrwst 2 or 3 miles from here.

While he was here I finished my drawing of roses for Mr [Penry] Williams & sent it by him. It was pretty. I gave Gibson a drawing of the mountains & have sent the view of Edinburgh for Mrs Lawrence which Mr Pidgeon helped me with. The pain in my arm now prevents my drawing much or I should have liked to have sketched a bit with him. Sometimes I feel sorrowful when I think I shall never draw again as I used to but I dismiss the regret & think how immeasurably higher & better & more lasting are the sources of heavenly joy than any earthly pleasure.

Saturday 30 August

…Robert Traill arrived…

2nd September

…On Saturday Gibson left with Harry who went that day to Liverpool. It was a very wet morning & they were obliged to go in the WChapel something going wrong with the wheels of the carriage. Gibson however was no worse & got safe to Lord Fitzwilliam's that day. - I suffer pain more, & can't do half I used…

Samuel Sandbach (1769 - 1851) was born in Tarporley, Cheshire, to Adam Sandbach and Martha Oulton. Samuel was a successful entrepreneur, becoming immensely wealthy. He married Elizabeth Robertson and had 10 children, of which Henry was the eldest surviving son. He passed away in 1851 in the presence of Margaret and Henry. Private Collection.

Samuel Sandbach (1769-1851) a anwyd yn Tarporley, Swydd Gaer, yn fab i Adam Sandbach a Martha Oulton. Roedd yn entrepreneur llwyddiannus a daeth yn ŵr hynod gyfoethog. Priododd Elizabeth Robertson a chawsant 10 o blant. Henry oedd y mab hynaf a oroesodd. Roedd Margaret a Henry wrth erchwyn ei wely pan fu farw ym 1851. Casgliad Preifat.

Tuesday 9th
Busy with home affairs Tidying up after the Artists & putting things in their place. Got things ready to go to Denbigh Flower Show tomorrow…

Astors, Hollyhocks, Roses, Viebenas, Fruits ----- a good show, gay but our flowers cut last night were dead. We got 3 2nd Prizes

September 14th
Sunday Evg Have just heard of the death of Thomas Roberts the clerk's son. We have watched him sinking for the past few weeks.

Oddi wrth Gibson at Margaret:

Thursday Oct 2nd
Morning - began to look over & arrange my passages about Gibson. - Am not so well this week, in consequence I think of arsenic medicine…

Saturday 4 -
Got on with my Gibson writing. Better today & in cheery spirits - less pain - feel happy & thankful.

His frame was quite worn out but his mind was clear & cheerful & I believe he was prepared for his death. How soon I may follow! His grave will be in the churchyard where I, too, will lie. Death is awful when we see it in others - it seems to come nearer to us than ever when we look forward to it ourselves, But in reality why should we dread it? It is truly said that our living as as wonderful & mysterious as our dying - that we are in reality as strange as that we shall be.

Gibson to Margaret:

September 27th 1851

My dearest Sis,
…your dear words of affectionate thoughts of me. On Monday morn we start onwards and in a few hours I shall see England once more receding in the distance, as the distance lengthens between us I feel that our souls draw closer together — anxious thoughts of you my beloved friend are constantly in my mind and will accompany my steps to every place.

When I arrive in Paris I will soon go to the Post in hopes of finding the dear hand — it follows me to every place — I am never forgotten…[5]

Tuesday 14 Oct
Drove to Pwllycrochan - saw Lady Erskine. A long shaky ride. And too much fall fanning for which I blame myself…

Yesterday October 18th [1851], the clouds were very fine at times, gloomy with sheets of light now and then. I went to throw away some dead flowers and returning to the front door I paused to watch a great white cloud that lay like a solid bank in the Eastern sky. It looked to me like a solid, heavy footing in the gloomy darkness

[5]Aberystwyth, National Library of Wales, MS 20566E-126. John Gibson to Margaret, 27th September 1851.

around, and I thought of heaven and earth where ion my heart and mind. When I heard a small voice calling me at the door 'where Ma-ga-dit! – Ma-ga-dit!' Sweet little voice raised to call me. 'Oh earth' I thought, 'sweet and alluring thou canst be yet!' I went in and the darling Eddie was at the door looking for me. Dear innocent darling there is about him a heavenly sweetness, a gentle inquiring expressive touch…

October Monday 20th
Copied some of my 'Gibsonia.'

22 October
…Fine outside but bad inside. Never passed a more disagreeable day. Did nothing but write a few notes and letters. Dear Edward

and Fanny left and I cried at the door…Had been weak and ready to cry all morning - overpowered all day - weak and miserable - ready to burst into tears every minute. Tried to be kind and smiled at people with an ache at my heart and a pain in my poor breast - oh me - the grave is a peaceful place - sometimes I am so tired.

October 23rd
…Less pain today. Not to go to London for 10 days - don't think it much signifies when they can do nothing for me. There is only one Physician can cure me and he deals with the Soul. I know I am dying and all I desire is to be left in peace at home and not to have to bear the gaze and questionings of strangers. Tho I ought to bear all things - oh so much better than I do. What a poor weak wretched creature I am….

From Gibson to Margaret:

Oddi wrth Gibson at Margaret:

28th October 1851

My dearest Sis,
If you received mine from Leghorn…you will not call me a forgetful good for nothing fellow…
Now I must tell you in reply to your last [letter] to Rome dated 15th October that this morning I at last found at home the German doctor – he said, first, in reply to my question – 'yes the first English doctor know every method of treating that disease that the Germans know' – there is no secret in the cure of it. I then read to him that part of your letter – he said, Brodie is the first man in England – no German can do more than he in such a case. He also remarked that the tumour when hard is smaller, its being a little larger was not a bad sign, it is when it softens it becomes larger. He observed that if the lady could come to a warm climate such as Italy it would be advantageous for that complaint.

Now Sis, don't you fancy that I put that into his head I give you my word of honour I did not. He also said that the Baths of Germany would be a very good thing I think he said the Baths of West Barden. It was from all he said that he considers you in the first rate hands – ['] then doctor you consider that this warm climate would be a good thing for her? – Yes, a very good thing for that complaint ['].

Perhaps Miss [Mary] Lloyd may come here, poor Miss Lloyd, I fear she is in a bad way…[6]

Benjamin Gibson, John's younger brother. Margaret records that whilst staying at Hafodunos during August 1851 'Poor dear Gibson rec'd news of Mr Ben's death. Harry broke it to him gently. We are so sorry…' Private Collection.

Benjamin Gibson, brawd iau John. Mae Margaret yn cofnodi, tra roedd yn Hafodunos ym mis Awst 1851 'Poor dear Gibson rec'd news of Mr Ben's death. Harry broke it to him gently. We are so sorry…'. Casgliad Preifat.

[6]Aberystwyth, National Library of Wales, MS 20566E-128. John Gibson to Margaret, 28th October 1851.

A miniature watercolour by Margaret, detailing a cow in the highland meadows above Hafodunos. Private Collection.

Miniatur mewn dyfrlliw gan Margaret yn dangos buwch yn y caeau uwchben Hafodunos. Casgliad Preifat.

Friday October 26th
…much pain this evening… Looking back on the past week is less happy to me than usual. And I find more cause than ever for penitence and prayer. I have been distressed, isolated and un-peaceful. Partly no doubt from my strength and spirit over cast by outward circumstances… I was jealous. A humiliating confession but this book is honest… Harry who I flattered myself would continue to put my comfort first. Should seem to think less of it and enjoy happiness with others while I was weary and depressed…

Tuesday 28th October
Left Chester at 1.45 and stayed the night at Stanley Place … Worcester …Cheltenham …London…

Saturday 1 November
Clifford St - good rooms and very snug. Dear Harry went to Mr Murray and got very kind and useful advice about my book - then went to see Bentley who took it and it is coming out soon! I am very glad it is settled, as I do hope it is in some degree worth publishing - I have felt better these few days past. At night we spent an hour or two with Mrs Huskisson who was kind and full of enthusiasm as ever.

Monday 3rd November
Saw Mr Hodgson. He found me worse. We are to come again by the 15th to see Brodie and consult. I was a little out of heart at first, but grow calm again soon and happy and did not lose all hold on Hope.

Wrth i'r gaeaf ddechrau brathu, ysgrifennodd Margaret at Dr Trail:

As winter took hold, Margaret wrote to Dr Trail:

13 Nov 1851

'My dear Dr.,
It is with very grateful and affectionate feelings that I receive your kind proposal about being present with me at that time. I had thought about it and had made up my mind to be quite alone, but that if I wished for anyone 'it should be Dr. Traill' – I knew you would come and had relied this upon you. And still do, if I feel the least wish or faltering or uncertainty, I will send to you, believe me. At present I keep firm to my wish to be alone, with only Hodgson & his attendant. Harry has agreed to this & my only anxiety is for him & to please him all I can. But, Dr dear, its not quite dire yet, whether it will be, or not - till after the consultation I conclude however it is most likely. God bless you love & thanks ever attend you, and Harry's too. He feel your kindness,

M Sandbach'[8]

[8]Powys Record Office, M/D/SAND/5/90
[9]Vere Street Chapel off Oxford Street, a continuation of New Bond Street.

Tuesday 4th November
Came home to dear Haf(odunos) by Express - I am glad to get here. Thank God for his many mercies. I am never out of his hands, and so, tho' worse in body I trust better in the Soul. Wrote poem for new book on my way from London…Wed 5th …Wet & Windy. Wrote letters. Got on with Gibson's work…

Sat 8th November
Clothing club sale. Did not go in beginning – went to part of the time…I finished Gibson.

November 10th
Monday, Tuesday, Wed, Thursday - all busy happy and days arranging things indoors - finishing copying Gibson's papers - getting done many little things.

Sat 15th November
Came to London by Express

Sunday - a little tired. Mr Hodgson came (after we had been at Vere St Chapel) & sat an hour with us.[9] Thought me no worse than last time. Proofs here.

Monday 17th November
Dr consultation at 2.30. Decided I had better have an operation. Kind Mr Hodgson will come again
tomorrow to hear all we may have to say….

Tuesday 18 November
Morning was correcting proofs when dear Harry carried me off in a 'Hansom' to Chiswick. Had a very nice ride and pleasant walk in the Gardens. Mr Hodgson came at 3 - most kind. He does not perform the operation himself - he says it wd be painful to him, but his friend Mr Stanley. It will be next Friday….

Wednesday 19th November
…we are quite quiet…

Thursday 20th November
Morning corrected proofs and wrote letters. After to see printings at Mr Schultzer's and saw my own MS. stuck up, much to my amusement. Liked seeing the printing. Mr Hodgson and Mr Stanley came at 9 and examined me, preparatory to tomorrow. Nobody could be kinder, more gentle than Mr Hodgson and we place perfect confidence in him - I thank God for giving us a good friend at this time and my dear Harry confides me to his care in great peace, and it lessens his anxieties Dearest Harry I grieve to grieve thee, This journal must stand still for some weeks - but I dare say my dear Harry will keep it for me. - I trust it please God to restore me after the operation which is to be performed tomorrow, that I may resume my usual habits in about 6 weeks - but I will not look forward confidently, only with hope, trusting in my merciful and everpresent God that he will bless the means used for my restoration, tho' it be only for a time - long or short may my life be spent in obedience to his will…

Evening Thursday 20th November. Perhaps these are the last lines I may write in my journal for some weeks. I trust, if it please God to restore me after the operation which is to be performed tomorrow, that I may resume my usual habits in about 6 weeks. But I will not look forward confidently, only with hope…Long or short, may my life be spent in obedience… may my love be more steadfastly fixed on things above… And may I grow more ready for death when it may come. I would express once more my deep and grateful sense of my many mercies… for my most precious and beloved husband, whose caring goodness to me non know but myself…For my kind and skilful Doctor now I may say is my good and faithful friend, for my true hearted and affectionate Williams who does so much for me…And take, beloved husband, and good friends, my earnest thanks and forgive the poor return I can make you.

Dr Thomas Stewart Traill (1781-1862). Thomas was friends with John James Audubon and William Roscoe, after having met a young Margaret the Traill family became close friends. It was to Dr Traill that Margaret would turn when diagnosed with breast cancer. Private Collection.

Dr Thomas Stewart Traill (1781-1862). Roedd Thomas yn gyfaill i John James Audubon a William Roscoe, ac ar ôl cyfarfod Margaret pan oedd hi'n ferch ifanc daeth y teulu Traill yn gyfeillion agos. At Dr Traill yr aeth Margaret am gyngor pan ganfuwyd bod canser y frest arni. Casgliad Preifat.

VII

'…I have been asking myself, what are the fruits of my long illness? What has it taught me?[1]

Juno, Queen of the Gods, sending forth Hypnos, God of Sleep by John Gibson. Sepia, bodycolour and pencil on paper. Private Collection.

Juno, Queen of the Gods, sending forth Hypnos, God of Sleep gan John Gibson. Sepia a gwaith pensil ar bapur. Casgliad Preifat.

Tra roedd Margaret yn wael, ysgrifennodd Henry'r dyddiadur gan gofnodi ei gwellhad araf wedi'r driniaeth i godi'i bron, hyd nes y gallodd hi ysgrifennu eto. Parhaodd Henry i gofnodi mân ddigwyddiadau'r dydd yn y tudalennau ar y dde, a Margaret yn llenwi'r bylchau mewn llawysgrif plentyn â'i llaw chwith. Mae prysurdeb gwanwyn 1851 yn llwyr wahanol i ymdrechion torcalonnus 1852. Daeth diwedd ar y partïon a'r dawnsio, a dechreuwyd ar holi mewnol oedd yn goresgyn y boen gorfforol barhaus, fel rhyw hypnosis oedd yn cyrraedd bron at berlewyg crefyddol iddi yno yn ei chartref Cymreig. Sylwodd y rhai o'i chwmpas ei bod hi'n goresgyn ei hunan corfforol ac yn canolbwyntio'n llwyr ar y bywyd tragwyddol a dedwyddwch ei hanwyliaid wedi hyn.

Henry partly completed the diary when Margaret was unwell, he wanted to record her illness post-mastectomy until she was able to write once again. Henry continued to fill in the minutiae of everyday life on the right-hand pages, while Margaret with childlike writing with her left hand fills in the gaps. She wrote using a pencil as it was too painful to dip her pen in ink. The contrast between the busy days of the spring of 1851 and the depressing struggles of 1852 are stark. Parties and balls end, and an inward search begins, rising above the enduring physical pain, in self-hypnosis, reaching an almost religious ecstasy, in the surroundings of her Welsh home. Those around her comment on a removal from the physical being, concentrating solely on the afterlife, and the future happiness of those she was to leave behind.

21st November
(Henry takes over the diary)

In the morning a late breakfast correcting proofs and finishing slippers for my mother…Nurse came before 1….Sent her into William. Mr Hodgson at 2. He passed into the Bedroom and did not return, by 1/2 past Mr Stanley and his pupil Mr Hewer, Dr Snow and Sir B Brodie had passed the same way - in a few minutes William came to say all was ready and she left me. I saw her again at 4 in bed - let me leave no record of that time - much sickness all night, towards morning fever - restless excitement which continues till morning - nothing can exceed the kind attention of the Doctors - they come 3 & 4 times a day and stay as long as they can do anything - this constant attention must be a great help to nature to recover the shock…

23rd November
Sunday morning at 8 went to the Communion service at St James. Margaret that evening able to join in the Lord's Prayer but have not troubled her with any reading…Williams and Mrs Bailey take turns at night. I sleep in the next room and get up each time to give medicines.

24th Monday
This morning at 4 the stomach refused the draft and I give no more - and slept till 9 … but find her changed - restlessness quite gone - very, very feeble, speaks in whispers - position instead of being a difficulty 'never was so comfortable.' The wound was dressed first on Sunday afternoon. Mr Hodgson got an air cushion for her back - told me this morning she had dreamed of Pasiflora.

[1]Powys Record Office, M/D/SAND/2/2. March 9th 1852.

Thursday 4 December - up to this time recovery said to be as great as usual - she has got daily to a couch for two days and has seen Wm Roscoe and Dr Roscoe. Sir B Brodie called today, yesterday and today - she has not been so well as before

6th Monday - not so well for the last two days - violent pain came on last night. Doctors up with her all night - call in Brodie at 12.30 - people think her better. 4 letters arrive for her this morning - in afternoon Dr Latham called in.

7th Sunday - quiet night as to pain but restless - no sleep - pain towards morning, but picked up in the day. Latham, Hodgson & Stanley make another examination this afternoon and decide that the pain is caused not by disease of any vital organ but by an Abscess which is comparatively manageable - the violent pain has not recurred beyond a slight twinge - she is wearied by the examination and sleeps.

8th Monday night between 6 & 7 Abscess opened by Stanley, Brodie & Latham present, after a day of wearing pain … she got relief - much exhausted

From Gibson to Henry:

Oddi wrth Gibson at Henry:

December 10th 1851

Dear Sandbach,
I am exceedingly grateful to you for writing to me for I became haunted constantly by the anticipation of the fate of the dear invalid – she has got through it – now for the hope of her strength – her recovery from the shock.

I do sympathise with all my heart with you – the account you give is hopeful. It was done in time and the most able hands. Will you do me the favour to write again I hope to hear of her improvement. I have a presentiment that her strength will keep up – I shall open your next [letter] with a trembling hand – with what pain I think of her!

I will write no more at present. I find that I wrote to Mrs. Sandbach on the 27th November acknowledging hers where she also mentions the parcel being sent to the Mc Crackens I hope it will come safe. I will write to Mrs. Sandbach when I [you] tell me when. I know she can't write to me for a long time.

Ever Yours Most Sincerely,

John Gibson

Mrs Sandbach's new book I must get…²

²Aberystwyth, National Library of Wales, MS 20566E-129. John Gibson to Henry, December 10th 1851.

John Abraham Tinne (1807-1884), eldest son of Philip Frederic Tinne and Secretary to the Dutch Ambassador in London, afterwards Deputy Secretary of Court of Policy, Demerara. He was one of the survivors of the wreck of the Rothesay Castle, a paddle steamer, which was lost in the Menai Strait in 1831, with a loss of 130 lives. Private Collection.

John Abraham Tinne (1807-1884), mab hynaf Philip Frederic Tinne ac Ysgrifennydd i Lysgennad yr Iseldiroedd yn Llundain, yna'n Ddirprwy Ysgrifennydd Llys Polisiau, Demerara. Roedd yn un o'r rhai a achubwyd o longddrylliad y Rothsay Castle, rhodlong a ddrylliwyd yn Afon Menai ym 1831 pan gollwyd 130 o bobl. Casgliad Preifat.

Wednesday 24 - Christmas Eve - no end of the remarks of kindness from friends. M[argaret] much better, able to walk about the room, and to dine with me - wound neatly contracting - what changes since last Christmas - it seems as if one years progress of the world was equal to many years for us.

Sunday 28 December
(Margaret again writing in her diary)

Once more, thank God, I am able again to hold my pen though feebly - I am able to enjoy this period of convalescence in my dear Harry's society and with a book or a chat with a kind friend. I have also to express my gratitude to my good and skilful Doctors, 4 in number, I may almost say 5 (for the young surgeon assisting was very kind) especially to Mr Hodgson, & Mr Stanley, who operated and has given my case continuing attention. I was indeed brought low but the Lord supported me, blessed be his holy name! I was too weak and suffering to think of Him but he did not forget me! Oh if I had not striven before this time to look calmly on suffering and death, what additional pain would have been mine! but blessed be God, my mind was calm and I knew my Soul was in His hands - so I lay passive. But since I began to get better and look on life, I wish to live, and some anxious thoughts will pervade? But I strive against them and perhaps being still so weak, little anxieties get more hold on me - I have suffered much and that

has perhaps shaken my firmness both of mind and body - but I will strive. And my own beloved Harry! of thy dear and never failing care what shall I say - oh silent must tongue and pen be, for they cannot tell it. Dearest God knows thy labour of love - it is enough. Thanks to all my kinds friends who have been so affectionately good to me. Dearest Emmes came all this way to see me. M. Tinne stayed from home and children for a fortnight to cheer us up, and she did cheer us. It was so pleasant to see my Emmes' face, my dear brother God bless him. Oh I have had such comfort, may I never forget this time and be ever grateful to God and to those he has given to love and tend me.

31st December
Last night of this old year, I look forward to the next with a strange mixing of feelings — hope and love and fear and desire to live more for that other would to which we all hasting oh if all I did but realise it more and that my faith was stronger and by him and then I might put fear out of my life. But often I dread that I may not be able to bear what may come and yet I have been brought through this 'Oh thee of little faith'. Save me oh lord from an unbelieving heart, forgive me of all my past sins. This gone year forgive my beloved one if he has ever disobeyed I bless thee for him my earthly treasure for his goodness in virtue and love.

From Gibson to Margaret:

Oddi wrth Gibson at Margaret:

Margaret Tinne (1811-1868), another sister of Henry's. She married John Abraham Tinne in 1833, a merchant of Liverpool and deputy-lieutenant and JP of Lancashire. Private Collection.

Margaret Tinne (1811-1868), chwaer arall i Henry. Priododd John Abraham Tinne, masnachwr o Lerpwl, dirprwy raglaw ac YH yn Swydd Gaerhirfryn, ym 1833. Casgliad Preifat.

January 1852

My dearest Sis,

I confess to you that I was surprised and delighted to see again the dear hand – sooner than I expected – I did not wait to read the letter at my studio but read it at once in the Greek Caffi [sic] where our letters come from the post. I was so delighted that tears came into my eyes – men are not to know this because it is unmanly. Instead of returning to my statues I went and walked with you in my heart along the Tiber and my soul was in constant conversation with you. I said you must think of paying your next winter here – the German doctor said to me that a warm climate is the most favourable for such complaints – think of the works – the poors [sic] of the skin are closed up in a cold climate – much more open in a warm talk to your doctor upon that subject. Your manuscript Vita came three days ago quite safe and Mr Smith the sculptor arrived two days ago and the new vols [Spiritual Alchemy] he brought safe which I shall soon begin to read…

I must now bid you goodbye, dearest friend, God bless you forever.
J.G.[3]

Sunday 4th January
1st Sunday in the New Year is always a very thoughtful day, and ought to be so. May the Lord impress upon our hearts the solemnity of life, of death, and of eternity, and bless our endeavours to do and bear his will.

I have not begun my journal till today, not being able to write much, and I have very little to record, my days being monotonous and not marked either by inward or outward events. This morning Harry was at Vise Street and this afternoon at Westminster Abbey. Mr Cardwell and Annie came to see me, and my Dr as usual. No one else.

5th Monday
Harry went to Rivers Gardens at Saidburyworth. Kind Mr Stanley came to take me out, but Harry being away we did not go. Corrected 'Spiritual Alchemy' as Mr Bentley thinks of printing again.

Wednesday 7th January
Got my new gown on - don't feel quite so fresh today. William Cardwell Roscoe came to see me and Mr Boxall came up with Harry from the Club tonight. Began 'Ravenscliffe'…

Thursday 8th January
Had our first drive in kind Mr Stanley's carriage, fine day and enjoyed it. Called at Mr Hodgson's. Saw Mrs Hodgson - very nice lady and some pictures and a bust of Sir R Peel by Noble - very like. Not much tired and all the better. Thank God and my kind friends.

Saturday 10th January
Went out again, round Regent's Park. Bright pretty day. Pleasant, but myself not so well, quite. Harry got a nice carriage. William Cardwell Roscoe called. Hodgson and Stanley.

[3]Aberystwyth, National Library of Wales, MS 20566E-130. John Gibson to Margaret, January 1852.

Sunday 11th January
Harry at Vere Street Chapel. Mr Scabell preached from 'thy Kingdom come' – a very edifying sermon. Dear Harry gave me such a clear account.

I felt better today and very sharp. But my 2 Drs came and saw fit to burn my wound with caustic and I am poulticed - but not so sore as I expected. Feel happy in Faith today and have had sweet talk with my Harry.

Monday 12th
Not quite so well. Mary and Richard Hilton called. Wrote some letters.

Tuesday 13th
Very poorly with fever

Wednesday 15th
In bed all day

Thursday 15th
ditto

Friday 16th
ditto
Dr Latham called in

Saturday 17th
Dr Latham came in the morning with Mr Stanley and found me better. Mr Hodgson came in the evening and met Mr Stanley

Sunday 18th
Slept all morning, felt poorly till Mr Hodgson came in the evening and gave me solid food which did me good; was wheeled into the drawing room in the evening. 'That they may show how true the Lord my strength is, and that there is no unrighteousness in him.' Psalm 92.14

Monday 19th
fever subsides, appetite commences to revive. William and John Tinne arrive with Anna bringing her to Lady Malkins, and leaving together next day to Belgium.

Tuesday 20th
slept 10 hours last night without waking and without the help of opiates - strength returning however very, very slowly.

Wednesday 21st
Symptoms of a gathering near the shoulder.[1]

Thursday 22nd
In bed all day, gathering increasing - great pain.

[Henry takes over the diary]

Friday 23rd
Gathering burst into the wound, profuse discharge - much relief. Mother (Mrs Sandbach) and Anne arrived at ½ past 4pm. Doctors pleased to find the abscess burst.

Saturday 24th
I drive with mother to look at a house and round Hyde Park, Green Park, Constitution Hill and the Houses of Parliament.

Sunday 25th
Morning at Vere Street Chapel, Mr Goulburn of Rugby preached. Afternoon, Westminster Abbey, Robert Trail dined with us. Margaret sat with us all evening.

Monday 26th
Busy looking for houses.

Tuesday 27th
Rain all day. Mother went to Harrow. M continuing better. Wrote to Mr Hoskyns about his house.

Wednesday 28th
Settled to take Mr Hoskyn's house and made preparations for moving to it.

Thursday 29th
Moved to the house No 3 Sussex Terrace Hyde Park Gardens.[3] Thank God for this first move

Mother went home on the 30th January by way of Cheltenham under the escort of Henry Harrison. Anne remained with us. Willie arrived on the 1st February and announced to us his engagement to Sara - Margaret continuing to improve.

I went to Hafodunos on Thursday 5th. I slept that night at Stanley Place and met Mr Palin at Haf. Mr John Wynne called on Thursday.

I remained at Haf til Monday 8th. Charlie Parker Junior came on Saturday and spent Sunday with me and his mother at Sussex Terrace. I went to Woodlands on Monday.

The 9th February to arrange with Willie to give up the Cottage to him, I returned to Sussex Terrace on Thursday 12th spending a few hours that day at Newton with Fanny and her 3 sweet children.

I find Margaret much increased in strength and we drove out on Friday 13th. Saturday was too cold to go out.

From Gibson to Margaret:

Oddi wrth Gibson at Margaret:

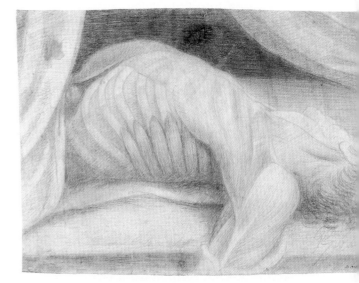

Half-length anatomical study of a man, drawn from a dissected corpse by John Gibson, circa 1815. Black chalk and graphite. Victoria and Albert Museum.

Astudiaeth anatomegol hanner hyd o ddyn, gan John Gibson, wedi'i dynnu o gorff marw dyranedig, tua 1815. Sialc du a graffit. Amgueddfa Victoria ac Albert.

12th February 1852

My dearest Sis,
…I feel the more grateful for a few lines written in your present state it is so great a proof of affection and of your thoughts of me. I was in hopes of your complete recovery. I suppose what you have now is a sympathetic infection from the original wound. I hope it will prove at the end beneficial to your constitution. I cannot tell you how delighted I am at the prospect of your return to Rome next winter… now, I will praise you after praising myself. I have read carefully your two vol[umes] which gave me great pleasure and the latter part of the two vol[umes] I thought rose up to high and beautiful sentiments and very powerful writing superior to your others. Williams has since read the work and greatly pleased yesterday[.] I lent them to Miss Blayden a poetess and friend of Barlowe's — perhaps I shall see her tonight at a Ball. When you come I will sit with you instead of going to parties.

…I am not yet sure about coming to England next summer, perhaps I may come and in that case I would return to Rome with you, it is steam all the way by land and ? from Paris to Rome and we may stop as often as you like on the way…

Please write three lines only to say how you are. I am so anxious to find you have got over this grave trial — God bless you.[4]

Sunday 15th February
Anne and I went to St Marys Church, Brynaston Square, Heard Mr Goring preaching confirmation. Drove out with M in the afternoon. Mr Hodgson and Stanley made appointment to make a minute examination of what they feared would be fresh tumours. They proved to be so and fixed to… 'you will never live to my age without you keep yourself in breath with exercise and in heart with joyfulness' if it be an old age says the man fond of hunting in Sir Philip Sydney's Arcadia.

Margaret Commented:

It seems I cannot say so: tho' I have more exercise than most women and have felt and cherished an uncommon share of

joyfulness of spirit. (for which I thank God; it being all his gift) — my life seems to be drawing to its earthly close and healthful exercises have only gave it cheerful and elastic for a time, till the awful hand of a fatal disease laid upon it…have a consultation with Sir B Brodie as to removing them.

Monday 16th February
Charles Parker arrived unexpectedly and took his wife to Harrow.

M and I drove out to Hopwood Gardens through the Squares, the Park, to Miss Callits and to Bridgeman's for cakes.

⁴Aberystwyth, National Library of Wales, MS 20566E-131. John Gibson to Margaret, 12th February 1852

Tuesday 17th February
The doctors met today - found fresh tumours - 4 external - decided to remove them at present - feared the cough might arise from one on the lungs.

Wednesday 18th February

Margaret:
Wrote to ask Turner to come up to London to meet Mr Hodgson and Stanley…happy bounding course. Still I would recommend to all women, the young especially, active out of doors pursuits. Enjoyment of open air, how intensely I have enjoyed these portions of my life, I can hardly describe. I do not regret now – these solemn moments, that much of it has been so spent. We are not always idlest when we seem to 'in villages and bye-lanes open eyes are always learning' – in gardens, fields and woodlands, we have be still at school' says Mr Wilmott.

Saturday 21st February
'lapis informatis'

Tumour burst. Charles Parker and M Tinne arrived in the evening to tea. Edward was also here. Anne left us to go with her husband to Euston.

Sunday 22nd February
Edward dined with us. M was at dinner and very well notwithstanding the burning. Charles, Anne and M Tinne came – pleased with Mr Hekker.

Monday 23rd February
Edward went home. Anne went to Torquay. M Tinne came to stay with us. Mr James Dixon also arrived having…

Sunday 29th February
This a fine bright breezy day. I am thinking how the sun is shining on my dear home – my heart is full of thoughts of that peaceful and lovely spot and hope of returning to it – full of

thankfulness to God for his mercies (and yet I feel how imperfect and inadequate my gratitude is) yesterday the doctors gave a more encouraging report and we are allowed to hope, if not for a cure, for a respite of the final sentence – for a period of alleviation and rest and the hope is pleasant to me and the having come from Chester on purpose to see us.

Tuesday 24th February
Tewson arrived to confer with Hodgson and Stanley. Consultation at 5. The same tumour burst again. The Dixons sat awhile. Strong east wind, clouds of dust.

Thursday 26th February
The Dixons went home. Willie came to breakfast, he was engaged in the city with the Demerara Railway and after with Snell furnishing the Cottage. I had influenza.

Friday 27th February
Willie still engaged in the city with Demerara Railway. My drive for life is still strong and the longing to fulfil and complete some wished for things at home (such as the new schools) rises in full force. But I dare not encourage these hopes – they are so uncertain! When I look at my dearest Harry and think, I may stay yet a little longer with him, the hope is too fond, too precious, to dwell upon it, and under the resignation I have been enabled to attain to – a week ago all was anxiety and complete hopelessness, it is the past week that has brought better symptoms – therefore they seem brighter for being unexpected.

And yet, what says St. Paul? That it is better to die part, and be with Christ.' In the afternoon brought Snell's plan and patterns. Mayant and M Tinne looked over them. Green came too with patterns of glass.

Saturday 28 February
Snell came in the morning much business settled with him. Early dinner that Willie and Mr Tinne might go home by express train.

Hodgson and Stanley met by appointment at 5 o'clock. Gave a somewhat encouraging report - the wound is healthy and the tumour that was burst is probably destroyed - the others not increasing - good hope of destroying them all.

Weather mild, east wind gone…death indeed release us, as we believe it does, from the pain and doubt and anxieties of earth, and usher us to the peace and joy and fulfilment of our father's house, our better home. Why do we wish to linger here? Why not desire first and chiefly to go there, to hasten there?

Why rejoice in what keeps us from it, why not hail every pain and pang that wears away this mortal coil, and helps to set us free? Alas! It is the weakness of our faith, the dimness of our spiritual sight. And God does not judge us harshly in this: we know out weakness, he has also implanted in us a love of present life, a certain clinging to 'the seen and temporal' which is not sinful and a leaning on the dear love that sweetens our earthly lot.

Tuesday 2nd March
We drove round the Park and walked in Kensington Gardens for Margaret to enjoy the air before being laid up - Stanley & Hodgson removed 6 Tumours - no chloroform - it was over about 2 o'clock - there is now no discoverable trace of the disease left - may it be permitted to heal without a return!

Mrs Huskisson called, also Mrs Cardwell and Captain and Mrs Molyneux.

Hodgson looked in again about 4 and again at 7 - doing very well - nothing done to the wound - a piece of dry lint put on it when she went to bed remains - she lost scarcely any blood. Stanley called at 1/2 past ten.

Monday 8th March
Margaret wrote: A very good street band played before our door. Looking from the window I was much amused to watch some children dancing to the music.

Two little girls bareheaded, but decently dressed were waltzing down the street joyous and graceful and one little child was capering away by itself and it made me laugh and felt quite merry to see it. It jumped and turned and twirled about as if it was possessed, and at last ran up a ladder and jumped down again. Oh happy gay things! Dance away – its short enough, your young joy.

I [Henry] dressed the wound. M kept her bed and saw no one.

Thursday 4th March
M still in bed all day but saw Mrs Wynne and Henrietta Roscoe.

Mr Hodgson dressed the wound.

Friday 5th March
Annie Caldwell called and saw M. No doctor came until 2 o'clock when Hodgson came and dressed the wound. Said he was going out of town till Sunday. Stanley called in, sat up in the bedroom the afternoon.

Saturday 6th
Harry dresses the wound in the morning and while he was out M came down stairs to the drawing room - imprudent. Stanley much surprised. I carried her up about 9 o'clock very sleepy and tired. I had been in the city and called on Mr Grayson and Howard.

March 9th
Margaret wrote: I have been asking myself, what are the fruits of my long illness? What has it taught me? How have I improved? Some good it was meant to do and I ought not to have thrown away so long a portion of time.

Sunday 7th March
M slept all night till after 8 o'clock - after breakfast I dressed the wound and went to church…

Miss Potts called and saw Margaret, also Boxall. Stanley dressed the wound at 5 o'clock - said it was doing well. I carried M down to the drawing room for the evening.

Monday 9th
Finished reading 'Head of a Family' – had a pleasant evening. I had been with Anne Caldwell in the morning to look at carriages.

Tuesday 9th March
Mr Hodgson returned and was much pleased with the state of the wound which he dressed in the morning, and Stanley in the afternoon …Mr Richard Phibbs called and sat with M. I still carry her up and down stairs. I dined at Mr Stanley's but came home early.

Wednesday 10th
Morning Mr Hodgson – Harry went out after lunch. I saw Mrs Dixon and Miss Potts. Annie and Jane Tinne – sweet creatures both.

From Gibson to Margaret:

Oddi wrth Gibson at Margaret:

10th March 1852

My dearest Sis,
I had been thinking of you every day lately… the sight of the dear hand delighted me…I am sorry you could not have sent me better news of your dear self. What is to be done! – still you say that your health is better – it is a great thing that you sleep well and a relief to be able to drive out. If you go to Hafodunos you will be removed from the doctors – but they will tell you when you can venture to retire from town. Your last book is liked here and soon I am going to lend to the sister and daughter and Mrs. Jameson who are here. They have read Hearts in Mort which I lent them and it gave them great pleasure.

…I shall be very anxious to hear how you get on – do not yet join the angels – we shall weep bitter tears whenever you do join them. How wrong of us! How difficult to conquer over nature!

Most Affectionately Yours,
John Gibson[5]

[5]Aberystwyth, National Library of Wales, MS 20566E-132. John Gibson to Margaret, 10th March 1852.

Mrs. Wynne of Coed Coch, near Abergele, whose gardens were greatly admired by Margaret. Courtesy of Auriol, Marchioness of Linlithgow.

Mrs. Wynne o Goed Coch, ger Abergele, oedd â gerddi a edmyguyd yn fawr gan Margaret. Trwy garedigrwydd Auriol, Ardalyddes Linlithgow.

Thursday 11th

Morning Mr Hodgson. Lucy Jevons and Harriet Roscoe came to see me. Saw no one else. Wrote many letters [using my] left hand about schools girls and Llanfair[taiharn] boys. Mr Stanley in the afternoon.

Friday 12th

Mr and Mrs and Miss Hodgson called in the morning but Williams dressed the wound. I went to the city. Stanley came in the afternoon. I saw Jane Lace who arrived from Chester.

Saturday 13th March

Laura Roscoe married. Mr Hodgson called. Saw Jane Lace here, William Caldwell Roscoe called and the Miss Stanley. Mr Stanley called but did not see the wound.

Sunday 14th March

Very cold day. Went to Westbourne Church… A quiet day together till afternoon when callers came: Mr Hodgson, Pidgeon, Audubon[6], Ray and Stanley.

Sunday 21st March

The week has passed as usual, I went to Torquay on Friday and returned on Saturday. I saw the nursery gardens at Exeter and got some rare plants.

Found on my return Margaret had been out - she was out again today - sent Williams to church and read the service at home.

Monday 22 March

The wound has been unhealthy for some days but nothing serious - some fresh treatment. Drove out today on the Harrow road. Busy making preparation to go to Hafodunos tomorrow. Rob Traill is to take care of M and Jane Lace will come and see her in the day time.

Sunday

Margaret wrote: Dearest Harry left for Hafodunos on Tuesday. I have spent a quick, flying week in spite of his absence. So many friends calling and so much kindness shown me in every way. Lady Eastlake sat an hour with me one day. Kind Jane Lace came every day and Annie Caldwell very often and Lady Russell with exquisite flowers – but I have been very poorly all week

March 29

Much better. Stanley quite pleased. We were out for a short time, too many callers. Mrs Haggett, Lady Russell, Miss Fupul, Jane Lace. The Tinnes on their way to the marriage at the Hague, flowers pour in from all directions, the finest are Colonel Clitheroe's roses.

Friday 2nd April Salt Hill

Alas, the cheerful promise of the last days note is not realised for the disease has again shown itself - for several days great pain in the shoulder - yesterday we left smoky dirty Sussex Terrace and in less than one hour were transported to this quiet cheerful place. M lay all evening on the sofa, in great pain which continued till mid-morning, when it ceased - the gathering apparently burst and today she does not leave her bed - is very happy listening to the birds and thinking of the blessings that still attend our lot.

Saturday

Mr Stanley came down in the evening and dined with us. Advised us to stay longer here.

Sunday 4th April

M remains in bed till afternoon. I went to Stoke Church. Gray's 'ivy mantled tower'. Hodgson came in the afternoon and dined with us. Applied laudanum to soothe the pain in the arms and 'twice' to the place.

[6]One of Audubon's sons.

116

Monday 5th April

Remained in bed till after 3 o'clock. I walked to Windsor. Still bright dry weather and east wind but not so cold today. Sun has great power.

Tuesday 6th April

Willie came on his way to Holland to be married. Mr Stanley and he dined with us and returned together to town. It was fixed that we remain here longer for a week. M walked in the garden for the first time.

Wednesday 7th

A bad night of pain until 2, after which sleep. The place presents a changed appearance, the tumour disappearing.

Too cold for M to go out. I walked to the Burnham beeches a little over 3 miles. Singular place, all the larges trees have at some time been pollarded and grown again. The underwood is chiefly juniper and some holly and very little gorse. Traces of abundance of fern in some places.

Thursday 8th April

I walked to Burnham. Mr Hodgson came. M very poorly

Friday 9th April

I went to London and engaged lodging at 64 Cambridge Terrace - found the plans for the school at Llangernyw at the Athenaeum. Margaret better.

Saturday 10th April

Left M pretty well and walked to Drosunnon, on my return found her very feverish

Monday 12th

Enjoyed being in the garden. Richard Hitton, Darcy and Sissie rode over from Englefield. Mr Watkin Wynne passed, on his way home from the stag hunt; everyone is pleasuring for the Easter holidays.

Tuesday 13th

Fine day, sent the servants off to London by the 11.52 train. We sat in the garden listening to the birds, dined early and came to Almonds by the 2.30 train - had the ground floor rooms which are the best.

Hodgson and Stanley met, thought the place so much better since Sunday that it did not look like the same person.

Friday 16th April

We all took the sacrament together. Gilbert, Williams, M and I. Gilbert and I went through St Bartholomews Hospital. Saw the dissecting room. Dined early. Lady Emily called , also William Roscoe and Jane Lace. We called in on Miss J Robertson and Miss Gladstone, also on Mr Jones the engraver, who has nearly finished my father's portrait. Saw copperplate printing at Ross and Dixons. Bought some summer dresses for Mrs Gilbert and spent the evening quietly.

Saturday 17th

We removed to our lodgings No 64 Cambridge Terrace Hyde Park. Mrs Pollard seems a decent Scotch lady and her house clean and comfortable. M suffering much pain, evidently gathering about the shoulder - lay all evening on the sofa – read letters to and from Jacob Fletcher. Mrs Tinne's account of the wedding. Read M's new book, containing the history of her childhood - very happy evening but pain coming on worse and worse when she comes to move. Could hardly get upstairs to bed.

Elizabeth Rigby, Lady Eastlake by David Octavius Hill and Robert Adamson, calotype, 1840s. National Portrait Gallery.

Elizabeth Rigby, Lady Eastlake gan David Octavius Hill a Robert Adamson, ffotograff cynnar, tua'r 1840au. Oriel Genedlaethol y Portreadau.

Saturday 17th April
M had a very suffering much pain evidently gathering about the shoulder - lay all evening in the sofa, read letters and M's new book containing the history of her childhood.

Sunday 18th April
M has had a very suffering night - gave her morphine at 4 which soothed her somewhat and towards morning she had a little sleep - has the gathering burst?

Monday 19th
Another painful night - the abscess really burst this morning about 10 o'clock - great exhaustion but peaceful rest follow.

From Gibson to Margaret:

Oddi wrth Gibson at Margaret:

Dearest Sis,
I have had in my heart pocket ever since I received it your last letter dated 29th March - it is a very short letter and I like it on that account, in your present state only five lines to say how you are getting on is enough. When you are re-established in health I hope your pen will run on at greater length.

…I was glad to find that you had not gone back to Wales but prolonged your stay… in London, me thinks the longer you are stay near the doctors the better at any rate for the present. I am always thinking of what you have gone through.

Mrs Wynne [of Garthewin] wrote to me and I have written to here… I also had a good and kind letter from Mr Penson but I have not written to him to tell him that Williams [Penry Williams?] and others as well as myself advise his drawing of Hafodunos.

…When I do come to England I shall be anxious to have a look at you and I am very anxious to hear of your strengthening – spero sempre…[7]

Wednesday 28th April
This day memorable in our domestic annals for a birth and a death recalls to me that I have neglected the diary, and indeed the days have been marked by nothing but the progress of disease and the cheerful endurance to beguile its weariness by writing 'Record of a Country House'. Yesterday Brodie, Lathom, Hodgson and Stanley had a long and anxious consultation. I hope our staying in London is now limited to a fortnight and that we shall go to Haf - today a feverish attack came on suddenly. I engaged Mrs Phillips as nurse to commence on Friday, and Williams is then to go and get Hafodunos ready for us.

[7]Aberystwyth, National Library of Wales, MS 20566E-133. John Gibson to Margaret, 23rd April 1852.

VIII

'…Her quiet eyelids closed - she had another morn than ours.'[1]

'I have often said that it is worth being born - to come into this world for the enjoyment of one sight of the starry heavens & of the ocean & then die' - Gibson[2]

Cupid carrying the sleeping Psyche by John Gibson, sepia wash and pencil on paper. Private Collection.

Cupid carrying the sleeping Psyche gan John Gibson, golch sepia a phensil ar bapur. Casgliad Preifat.

Under his wings thou shalt trust

Father, to thee I turn and cry,
Oppressed with sin and grief;
From the world's chilling air I fly,
Of thee to ask relief.

My soul would rest on thee, oh God!
Would shroud itself in thee;
Dark is the path my feet have trod;
Pity and pardon me!

I had no staff on which to lean,
No hand to guide aright;
Lonely and sad my life has been,-
Oh give me of thy light!

My God, I am a bruised reed,
A torn and bleeding heart;
I come to thee in deepest need,
O, take my mournful part!

Hide, hide thy stricken child of dust,
In thee let me repose;
My anguished, breaking spirit yet
No consolation knows.

Oh tender Father! on thy breast
With penitential tears,
I come to seek a holy rest,
A shelter from my fears.

But Thou art just!- oh dare I come?
Lord, turn not thou away-
Take the poor erring wanderer home,
Never again to stray.

Oh merciful! I meet thine eyes-
Thine arms outstretched to save;
I feel my sinking soul arise
Out of the whelming wave.

The angel of thy presence here,
Folds me beneath his wing;
And sheds on me the holy tear
Of his pure pitying.

Earth's beating storms for me are past-
Upon his breast I lay
My weary head. And peace at last,
Breaks o'er my darkened day.[3]

[1]The Death Bed, Thomas Hood (1798-1845).
[2]Powys Record Office, M/D/SAND/2/1. Note in endpapers of 1851 diary.
[3]Margaret Sandbach, 'Under his wings thou shalt trust', Aurora and other poems, (London: Pickering, 1850), p.22-3.

Margaret's passing was much rehearsed in her mind, her life a rehearsal for her death. The summer and winter of 1851 was a full dress rehearsal, during which Margaret set out all her plans. But she had been learning her lines for many years:

Roedd Margaret wedi ystyried ei marwolaeth droeon, roedd ei byw yn baratoad i'w marw. Bu haf a gaeaf 1851 yn ymarfer llawn o'r hyn oedd yn anochel, a gosododd ei holl gynlluniau'n fanwl. Bu hi'n ymarfer ei rhan ers sawl blwyddyn.

Guthrie, the loyal and beloved head gardener at Hafodunos. He worked closely with Margaret in designing the gardens around the old mansion house.
Courtesy of Auriol, Marchioness of Linlithgow.

Guthrie oedd y prif arddwr ffyddlon a hoff yn Hafodunos. Cydweithiodd yn agos â Margaret wrth gynllunio'r gerddi o amgylch yr hen blasty.
Trwy garedigrwydd Auriol, Ardalyddes Linlithgow.

Hafodunos, 18th May 1845

Grieve not, we shall soon meet again!

My dearest brother,
If I die before you, you must read this letter. It [the letter] is written in no light...
I have lived for many years, I may say nearly all my life, but especially lately, with a constant feeling of the utter uncertainty of life. Death has seemed to me to be 'at the door'. I have counted upon nothing on earth – I look forward from year to year to a vague something that may never come – the end of my earthly life is before me continually. I have grown familiar with the thoughts of death. And yet, my dearest, it is strange that this had not all its influence with me in leading me to a constant and steadfast preparation for that eternity which seems so near. Oh that we would work which it is day, never being that 'the night cometh when no man can work.'

Now let me speak to you while yet I can on earth while my long-cherished affection for you beats in a living breast, and listen to me my dearest – think that my voice is speaking to from that awful shade which we all must pass through! Search the scriptures and believe in Christ. It is our only true place on earth, our only anchor of Hope beyond the grave.

You have had many a struggle in your life – care and trouble lighted early on your young head, but an upright heart, and the love of friends (of one at least who after the death of parents loved you if possible more than ever) has lightened the clouds...forget not our early days – the purity of strength of our innocent affection, which never faltered. I have prayed for you and loved you to the last...[4]

[4]Powys Record Office, M/D/SAND/4/3. Margaret to Edward Henry, 18th May 1845.

Under his wings thou shalt trust, Psalm 91, drawing by Gibson, showing Margaret under the protection of an angel, dated 1841. Private Collection.

Under his wings thou shalt trust, Salm 91, lluniad gan Gibson yn dangos Margaret dan ofal angel gwarcheidiol, dyddiedig 1841. Casgliad Ppreifat.

Death was at hand, and Margaret sensed that her time was limited. In her journal, she began to comment on what the ending of her life meant, and how she would rationalise the process of transitioning from a physical plane to that of eternal life.

Roedd ei marwolaeth gerllaw, a synhwyrodd Margaret fod ei dyddiau'n dirwyn i ben. Yn ei dyddiadur, dechreuodd nodi ystyr terfyn ei bywyd, a sut y byddai'n rhesymoli'r symud rhwng ei bodolaeth gorfforol at y bywyd tragwyddol.

'Reflection on the prospect of Death'

'Oh Lord my best desire fulfil, and help me to resign life, health and comfort to thy world and make thy pleasure mine.'

June 27th 1851

Hymns are a great comfort; like single texts of scripture. They rise to the mind readily and kindly as it were, and help us to express our laden thoughts. And to one who loves the music of poetry, there is something soothing in their flow. The first certain appearance of the critical state, that we are in immediate jeopardy, is overwhelming at the moment, although we may have endeavoured to prepare ourselves for it. It changes at once the whole aspect of things to us; we look with quite a different eye on everything. No one can understand this quite who has not been so situated, either in immediate illness or the prospect of this fatal order. But I was surprised how much the blow was softened to me, how quickly and calmly my mind passed from an unquiet state of doubt and perplexity caused by the mingling of hope and fear, into the certainty to all earthly hope was over - what some would call despair — but what it really is, is an acknowledgment of God's awful presence and power. A surrender of our feeling to his divine will. In this, very likely there is something of the resignation that those to inevitable degree, a resignation difficult to submission and lower, far in the scale of spiritual life. But the soul advances from her first simple reception of the command, and begins to find grace in the dealing and to say… "Thy will be done," but I desired to do it in the ways those would have me and to use this, thy dispensation to its right and holiest and fullest purpose. And we soon… with our eyes opened to behold our greatest dealings, see how much we regarded chastisements and how fitted they are to our state and how purified and blessed we may be in the end. After passing through the refiner's furnace. How many happy and blessed things that are to us in this remnant of life on earth… How apt have we been in the full possession of life and hope and health to float down the sunny tide unthinking – and forget our haven. Now we are all out of the danger. We bear the cross and we are following our master…Oh sweet earthly love and sweet earthly home and many comforts, steal not away our thoughts from heaven. Smooth not my path too much.

Sometimes my faith is dead and cold and I question everything, and though composed and even cheerful, no happy light from heaven seems coming – nothing to cheer me. I am only resigned not thoughtful. I said this frame of mind will sometimes seem and that I must not be distressed, but try to wait happily… The grave looks cold and dark and God far away, this earth inviting rest… The mystery of the future presses upon us… The raising of that fail beneath which we must pass and be lost to earth forever… Some days are necessarily less hopeful and happy than others. Sometimes the remembrance of my certain state comes like a cloud over the sunshine of a happy talk with my dearest or a bright look into the garden and some little plan we may have projected about our home. And then, but it is not often, I lay my head on his dear breast and sigh a quick weep or tear – but he comforts me and all is right again. Then at night sometimes warmly crouching by his side I shudder for a moment to think of leaving him…..And go… this body to the cold grave – this spirit to unknown worlds – oh God, then it seems hard to part. We are human and love and life are strong within us!…

11th May Tuesday
We reached home yesterday in the Woodlands' carriage fitted with a bed. Mr Hodgson had come with us to Newton on Saturday where we rested on Sunday and Jenison came with us from their home - we reached home with wonderfully little fatigue - Mr Thomas came to Newton by invitation and administered the sacrament to us. M was much comforted by our uniting in this service and is very happy, able to look forward with a kind of joyful triumph to the approach of the last evening - nothing but a strength from above is sufficient for this. She is very glad to get home, to see Guthrie and Jane and to talk about the garden and the school, and is preparing two little girls in school to go to service but her interest is less vivid in all things - rest seems to be her greatest enjoyment - how great must be the enjoyment of the 'perfect rest' that remaineth for the people of God!

Thursday 13th May
Dear M slept badly last night - each day seems a labour to get through - she came down stairs after 2 o'clock, was out half an hour in the garden, slept on the sofa and then to bed. Jane is busy getting the girls ready for service, Guthrie planting out - he went round with us today - how glad he seemed to pull each favourite little flower that caught her eye but oh, how evidently the pain of weariness overcame her intense delight in looking on the garden - after dinner she had her head upon my shoulder and looked at the bright gleams from the setting sun that lighted up the young foliage and the green banks.

Friday 14th May
Yesterday was as a blank page - she was sick in the morning and when that subsided she slept all day and did not leave her bed. Today she has been better. She came down stairs between 2 & 3 - saw Mrs Wynn, sat with me at dinner but by 8 o'clock seemed to be quite exhausted. I carried her to bed - she complained of shortness of breath and pain in the chest - applied a belladonna plaster - wound very sore - felt chilly - but without sleep she becomes daily weaker.

Willie and Sara came on Saturday 15th and remained till Monday. Anne and Eliza came on Monday 17th.

Mr Turmeau was here on Monday morning - he burned the place, found it enlarged, gave tonic with a wonderful effect. M[argaret] was so much better that she got up and went into the garden, sat in the greenhouse, round the west walk, was out altogether 2 hours - did not sleep well at night.

Today Tuesday 18th May, very sick and weak, feeling oppressed, breathing short, she remained in bed all day.

Wednesday 19th May
Took Eliza to the station and bought mother and May Roscoe back. M came downstairs to receive them.

Thursday 20th May
She slept last night 10 hours without morphine, but was not refreshed - went in the chair to the garden down the dingle and up the carriage road, enjoyed listening to the birds, almost too happy.

Friday 21st May
Mr Turmeau came, found her very weak and poorly, anxious to give tonic, did not apply caustic - afternoon she drove in the Brougham up the hills to see the mountains - a fine day but very hazy - the carriage too uneasy. Will not use it again.

Saturday 22nd May
A good night but very sick in the morning - did not leave her room today but dressed to receive Mr Stanley who offered us a visit and I went to Abergele to meet him when the express stopped he was not there.

Sunday 23rd May
Brought a letter from Mr Stanley explaining that the little girl whose leg he cut off could not spare him. We hope he may come some other time. Mr Turmeau came as we came out of Church, and in the afternoon he and I took Margaret into the garden when she sat in her chair and enjoyed the air.

Monday 24th May
a weary day - much sickness in the morning. M never left her bed. Annie arrived, May Roscoe left.

Tuesday 25th May
M slept last night - natural sound sleep but wakened twice with violent pain in her head which gradually subsided. She has been somewhat better today - no sickness - more appetite. Annie left us. - we all went out in the afternoon - we got as far as the poultry yard, the cattle yard to see the Indian Calf and Brynview to see the mares and foals.

Wednesday 26th May
Only sat up to have the bed made.

Thursday 27th May
M very weak, and being a cold day she did not go downstairs but moved into Anne's room for a change - drove my mother and Anne in the Whitechapel up to the farm to see the improvements.

Friday 28th May
Another sunless day, but less wind - poor Margaret more and more weak - was carried in a chair in the afternoon from her bedroom into the garden - got as far as the seat under the Laburnam? and admired the view. Mrs Wynn came and sat with her in the garden. Turmeau was here this morning. I rode with him over the farm…

Saturday 29th May
Letter from Mr Stanley to say he will come today. The carriage that took my mother to Abergele brought back Mr Stanley, Mr Parker and Margaret Parker. We were all pleased to see Mr Stanley and it cheered our patient especially.

Sunday 30th May
Mr Turmeau came to breakfast after which was a consultation - there was a long visit to the sick room and some new treatment, all together it was a good day. Mr Stanley left us to go with Mr Turmeau to Denbigh to visit a patient intending to return to London by the night mail. We all went to afternoon church and in the evening Margaret came to the library. Mr Stanley walked the garden round with us and saw Thomas Rogers. Says he is too old even to be strong again, but he may really for a time. At night Margaret became very restless - obtained rest at length by means of opiate which resulted in a very exhausting sickness in the morning.

Monday 31st May
Too poorly to be dressed - lay dozing all day till 3 o'clock - better towards evening but has taken very little food all day. Charles Parker left us by the evening train. Very cold with hail showers and sunshine between.

Sunday 6th June
This has been a week of much weakness and the disease has made rapid progress - she is confined to her room but occupied when able as usual in thinking of others, and once in dictating for a few minutes - this morning she sang as she lay in bed - her cheerfulness is marvellous - a great blessing for which we cannot be too thankful. Ed Roscoe, Fanny and Eddie came on Friday - she has been giving them some keepsakes, among other things some of the baby cloths which she and Edward wore.[1] Mr Hodgson came from London yesterday and stays till tomorrow - the Express stops for him at Abergele station - it takes him about 10 hours from his house to Hafodunos - he looks pale. He gave Margaret some medicine that procured her a good nights rest.[2]

Oddi wrth Gibson at Henry: Gibson to Henry:

6th June 1852

Gibson was heading to London.
'…I am grieved to find the unsatisfactory state of the dear sufferer – our anxiety is still kept up – she bears
all with much resignation. It is impossible to contemplate her in her dreadful illness without being deeply
impressed by her greatness of mind – a soul beautifully calm under bodily sufferings…'5

Wednesday 16th June
An interval of comparative rest and comfort gives me time to record this book which has been neglected because all my time has been devoted to watching the deathbed of my dear wife and endeavouring to smooth her pillows and relieve her restlessness. No pain strictly she has scarcely any and the peace of mind is both a lesson and a comfort to us all instead of requiring and external help. To begin were I left off last on Monday, Mr Hodgson and the Roscoes and Mr Parker all left us.[3]

On Tuesday Mr Turmeau did not come[4] - he came and went on Wednesday the 9th - after he was gone and after we had just sat down to lunch the nurse came hastily to summon us to the sickroom, she said there had been a slight convulsion. We found M much excited with difficulties of breathing which continued some

hours and left her in a very exhausted state. This sort of attack has recurred two or three times, and we have all thought on each occasion that her death was near at hand - she has sent kind messages to absent friends, given such directions as occurred to her about her worldly affairs - and then we have sat around her reading at intervals comforting texts or hymns - or repeating those of which she gave us the first words but had not breath to repeat - we have frequently joined in prayer and in commending her spirit to our heavenly father - this with the needful attention to her physical wants has occupied us night and day, taking by turns to watch and sleep. Turmeau came over every other day, each time not expecting to see her again. This afternoon Wednesday 16th she seems better than she has been for some days, dozing a good deal and breathing more freely and she has taken leave of Mr Palin. Thomas Rogers is very ill in the village, not likely to be better

5National Library of Wales, MS 20566E-134. John Gibson to Henry, 6th June 1852.
6National Library of Wales, MS 20566E-135. John Gibson to Henry, 21st June 1852.

Gibson to Henry:

Oddi wrth Gibson at Henry:

Gibson designed Margaret's memorial in the church yard of St. Digain's, Llangernyw.
Photographed by Antonia Dewhurst.

Gibson gynlluniodd y gofadail i Margaret ym mynwent eglwys Sant Digain, Llangernyw.
Ffotograff gan Antonia Dewhurst.

My dear Sandbach,

I arrived here this morning and am anxious to hear from you. I would come down just to see the poor sufferer if you think she is in a state to be visited by me – I fear that she is in a very fragile state - I shall be regulated by your judgment.

I mourn deeply over your great misfortune.
Ever yours,
John Gibson[6]

Henry's desolation was both profound, and exhausting, having borne witness to his wife's disease and drawn-out death. For years to come, he was unable to let go of her memory. He wrote in the wake of Margaret's death:

Roedd trallod Henry yn ddwfn a lluddedig, wedi iddo fod yn dyst cyson i waeledd ei wraig a'i marwolaeth hirfaith. Am flynyddoedd i ddod, methodd â'i rhyddhau o'i feddwl. Yn sgil marwolaeth Margaret, ysgrifennodd:

'One of the last things she said to me was 'there is one thing I wished that I have not been able to do, to make you three drawings to hang in your dressing room. One of the church where I shall be laid, one of the mountains [where] we have so often delighted ….together, and one of a little daisy that is me, a little thing lying so close to the ground but looking up [to] heaven and gladdened by the brightness there… No this was not said to me, I find it in her letters. '

Wednesday 23rd June - printed cutting -

'We watch'd her breathing thro' the night
Her breathing soft and low
As in her breast the wave of life
Kept heaving to and fro.
So silently we seemed to speak
So slowly moved about,
As we had lent her half our powers
To eke her living out.
Our very hope belied our fears,

Our fears our hopes belied -
We thought her dying when she slept
And sleeping when she died.
For when the morn came dim and sad,
And chill with early showers,
Her quiet eyelids closed - she had
Another morn than ours.
surrounded by a bold black box -
On the 23rd June about half past
one a.m. my Margaret expired
in her sleep

129

IX

Above and opposite: The immortal Margaret, resplendent in stained glass at St Digain's Church, Llangernyw. Author's Collection.

Uchod a chyferbyn: Yr anfarwol Margaret, yn ysblennydd mewn gwydr lliw yn Eglwys Sant Digain, Llangernyw. Casgliad yr Awdur.

A Lamentation

It weighs upon my heart, my love,
  It weighs upon my heart,
To think that thou art lost to me
  Beloved as thou wert!
It haunts me in the evening hour,
  And in the morning light,
That never more thy cherished form
  Shall bless my longing sight!

It weighs upon my heart, my love!
  It weighs upon my heart,
To think that when all else was bright
  We should be forced to part!-
In vain for me thy garden smiles,
  In vain the balmy air;
The flowery paths are desolate-
  Thou art not with me there!

I cannot shake the burden off!
  It clings unto my soul;
Upon the sighing winds I hear,
  I hear deathbell toll-
I see a pointed arrow fly-
  'Tis death's unerring dart!

Giuliano De'Medici – A Drama- With other poems 1842

132

'The old school, enlarged in 1844, has been taken down and a new architectural but smaller one erected, with a master's house attached. In the schoolroom is the following inscription upon the wall; - This School is dedicated to the Memory of MARGARET SANDBACH, in remembrance of her pious and unswerved labour, to promote the moral and spiritual culture, as well as the social advancement of her neighbours. She died at Hafodunos while the building was in progress...[1]

A beautiful painted window has... been put up in the south transept of the church: - 'In memory of MARGARET, wife of Henry R Sandbach, of Hafodunos, who died June 23rd 1852; erected by subscription as a memorial of her abundant kindness, especially to the poor of this parish.' The lower lights of this window are filled with four full length female figures representing Faith, Hope, Charity and Humility. The tracery or upper compartment is filled with emblematic representations of the person of the Holy Trinity, all of which have been well and tastefully executed by Mr Ballantine of Edinburgh.'[2]

Emotions after Margaret's demise were raw. Her nephew, William, was moved to compose a poem in the days following his vigil at her deathbed:

Roedd emosiynau'n gignoeth wedi marwolaeth Margaret. Cafodd ei nai, William, ei ysbrydoli i gyfansoddi cerdd yn y dyddiau wedi'i wylnos ar echwyn ei gwely angau.

M. S.

Like morning, or the early buds in spring,
Or voice of children laughing in dark streets
or that quick leap with which the spirit greets
The old revisited mountains - some such thing
She seemed in her bright home. Joy and delight
And full eyed innocence with folded wing,

Sat in her face, and from her happy smiling
Clear air she shook like starlit summer night,
What needed pain to purge a spirit so pure?
Like fire it came - what less than fire can be
The cleansing Spirit of God? Oh, happy she
Able with holy patience to endure!
Her joy made peace, and those bright orbs of nature
Subdued to purest gold of piety

[1] A short sketch of the life and character of the late Mrs Sandbach, Hafodunos - Marwnad i'r diweddar Mrs Sandbach, Hafodunos, gyda nodiadau ae ei bywyd a'i chymeriad, Robert Hughes author of 'Ancient and Modern Denbigh' (Robyn Wyn o Eifion) University of Wales Bangor DG323

[2] A short sketch of the life and character of the late Mrs Sandbach, Hafodunos - Marwnad i'r diweddar Mrs Sandbach, Hafodunos, gyda nodiadau ae ei bywyd a'i chymeriad, Robert Hughes author of 'Ancient and Modern Denbigh' (Robyn Wyn o Eifion) University of Wales Bangor DG323

'…At her own request, her remains lie interred in the open Church yard at Llangerniew [sic], where a neat monumental pillar bears the laconic inscription 'MARGARET SANDBACH, 1852'…'[3] Antonia Dewhurst.

A hwythau eto yn eu gwewyr cyntaf, ystyriodd Gibson a Henry sut orau fyddai ei choffáu.

Still in the first throes of loss, Gibson and Henry considered how best to preserve her memory.

14th July 1852

Dear Sandbach,

I postponed writing to you to say how much pleased I am to find that you sanction my wish to erect a memorial in some church in L.pool [Liverpool] – when I do go there I should wish much if you could join me there to see what place may be had. When the time comes I will let you know. I would rather not come to Hafodunos this year – it would be very painful to me to come there just now.

London
1852, July 28

Dear Sandbach
Many thanks for the favour of your last. I approve very much the your ideas of building a place at Hafodunos for the statues – in memory of her – perhaps I may prefer to my memorial placed among the statues instead of a church at L.pool [Liverpool], but when we meet we can settle this point.

I have been making a slight sketch of the monument which I shall bring with me to show you and family… it is a figure of herself.

I saw a granite grey square monument, which I like very much – it had a vase on the top. '…a square form agrees with her own idea…'[4]

Clodforwyd ei bywyd gan awduron a beirdd ynghyd â sut y dioddefodd ei diwedd hirfaith a phoenus.

Authors and poets praised her life and the way in which she endured her painful, drawn out demise:

'…having, under great bodily affliction, evinced exemplary patience and resignation, and met death with an astonishing degree of Christian fortitude.'[5]

[3]A short sketch of the life and character of the late Mrs Sandbach, Hafodunos - Marwnad i'r diweddar Mrs Sandbach, Hafodunos, gyda nodiadau ae ei bywyd a'i chymeriad, Robert Hughes author of 'Ancient and Modern Denbigh' (Robyn Wyn o Eifion) University of Wales Bangor DG323
[4]National Library of Wales, MS 20566E-127. John Gibson to Henry, 28th July 1852.
[5]Robin Wyn O Eifion, A Short Sketch of the Life and Character of the late Henry Sandbach, 1856

Henry remarried in 1855, some three years after Margaret's passing. But he remained wedded to her memory. His second wife, Elizabeth Charlotte Williams of Bryngwyn, near Welshpool was in her early 30s and a wealthy heiress, had met Henry during his time as High Sheriff of Denbighshire.

Ail briododd Henry yn 1855, rhyw dair blynedd wedi marw Margaret. Ond roedd yn gyson ffyddlon i'w choffadwriaeth. Roedd ei ail wraig, Elizabeth Charlotte Williams o Bryngwyn, ger y Trallwng yn ei thri degau cynnar ac yn etifeddes gyfoethog. Roeddynt wedi cyfarfod gyntaf pan oedd Henry yn Uchel-Siryf Sir Ddinbych.

Henry and his family in later life. Left to right: Samuel, Arthur Edmund, Henry Martin, Margaret, Henry, Sophy and Elizabeth Charlotte Sandbach, circa 1870. Private Collection.

Henry a'i deulu newydd. O'r chwith i'r dde: Samuel, Arthur Edmund, Henry Martin, Margaret, Henry, Sophy ac Elizabeth Charlotte Sandbach, tua 1870. Casgliad Preifat.

Cofnododd Elizabeth Charlotte yr achlysur o godi'r gofeb i Margaret:

Elizabeth Charlotte records the erection of Margaret's monument:

1856

Thursday 21st August - John Hughes placed Gibson's monument to Margaret in the niche in the little room. Henry could not wait longer for Gibson's uncertain visit. I watched it being placed with great interest & anxiety. I love to gaze upon it, to learn her character from its features, & trust I may make my Harry as happy through many long years as she did. There is something so elevating & life inspiring in all connected with her that I like to cultivate every means of her memory living among us. Nothing gloomy can belong this spirit.

1857

Tuesday 1st September - Met Gibson…So glad to make Gibson's acquaintance. I feel he quite belongs to Margaret at Hafodunos & until I know all her friends I do not feel to belong to him.

Dechreuodd Henry ar waith chwe blynedd i ail adeiladu ei gartref priodasol ac oriel gerfluniau fel cofadail parhaol i'w wraig gyntaf. Y pensaer gafodd y gwaith cynllunio oedd neb llai na Gilbert Scott. Roedd Scott yn bensaer toreithiog, gan gynllunio, neu fod â rhan yng nghynllun, wyth gant o adeiladau yn ystod ei yrfa. Pan dderbyniodd y comisiwn hwn, roedd eisoes wedi'i benodi yn bensaer yn Abaty Westminster ac yn fuan wedyn byddai'n cynllunio gwesty'r Midland Grand yng ngorsaf St Pancras a'r gofadail odidog i'r Tywysog Albert ar gais y Frenhines Fictoria ei hun. Byddai Hafodunos a'r oriel gerfluniau yn benodol, yn gofadail i Margaret gan Henry (ac unig gomisiwn Scott i gynllunio adeilad preswyl yng Nghymru).

Henry embarked on a six-year project to rebuild the marital home and sculpture gallery as a permanent memorial to his first wife. He entrusted the design to no less an architect than Gilbert Scott. Scott was an extremely prolific architect, designing partly or wholly eight hundred buildings in his career. At the time of the commission, Scott had already been appointed architect at Westminster Abbey and was later to erect the recently restored Midland Grand Hotel at St Pancras Station and the magnificent Albert Memorial for Queen Victoria herself. Hafodunos and the sculpture gallery in particular, was to become Henry's memorial to Margaret (and Scott's only residential commission in Wales).

Gibson's design for the sculpture gallery at Hafodunos. National Library of Wales.

Cynllun Gibson ar gyfer yr oriel gerfluniau yn Hafodunos. Llyfrgell Genedlaethol Cymru.

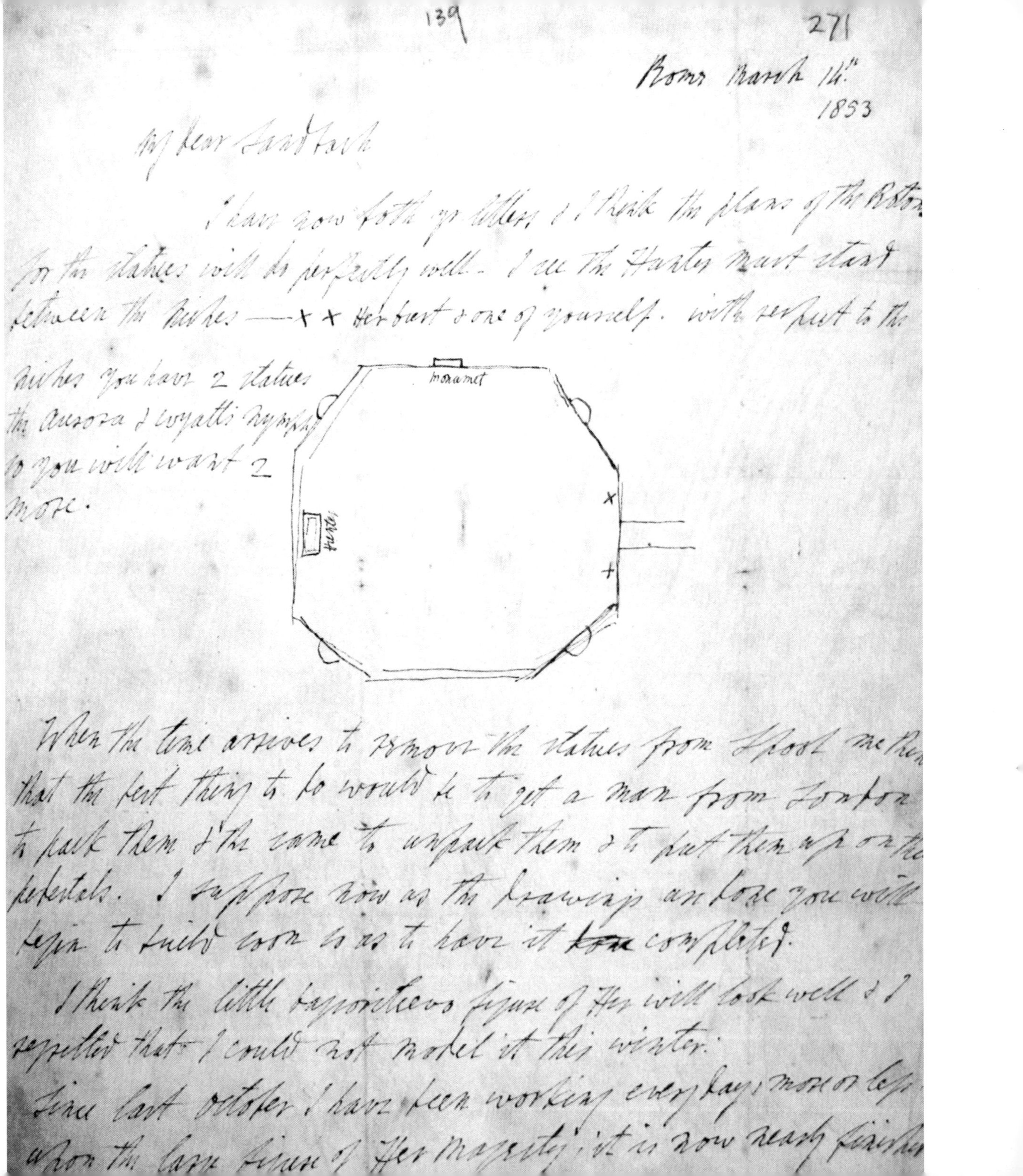
139

271

Rome March 14th
1853

My dear Sandbach

I have now both yr letters & I think the plans of the Rotonda for the statues will do perfectly well. I see the Statues must stand between the niches — × × Herbert & one of yourself. with respect to the niches you have 2 statues the Aurora & Wyatt's Nymph so you will want 2 more.

When the time arrives to remove the statues from Lpool methinks that the best thing to do would be to get a man from London to pack them & the same to unpack them & to put them up on the pedestals. I suppose now as the drawings are done you will begin to build soon so as to have it ~~done~~ completed.

I think the little baptismal figure of Her will look well & I regretted that I could not model it this winter.

Since last October I have been working every day more or less upon the large figure of Her Majesty, it is now nearly finished

The construction was monumental and was to include an imposing clock tower and was to be everything that the old home was not. Gone was the Welsh vernacular design, nestling into the hillside. This was an ultra-modern home, whose design employed the latest construction methods and used materials gathered from abroad.

The sculpture gallery was entirely rebuilt and given pride of place; it was the first part of the new home to come into view on the main approach. This octagon was the inner sanctum where the intense trio were to immortalise their complex relationship; the sculptures by Gibson, the gallery itself commissioned by Henry; and all inspired by Margaret. In this temple, Henry's and Margaret's busts were placed facing one another. While we know Gibson had sent a plaster bust of himself to Hafodunos, there is no evidence of Charlotte ever being so memorialised.

Henry consulted closely with Gibson on the exact siting of the house and the design of the memorial gallery. Margaret was a constant presence in the lives of the men whom she had loved during the entire construction period. Henry's diary is peppered with entries that reveal how preoccupied he remained, even years later, from weekly visits to her grave, along with his wife Elizabeth, to the birth of a daughter. Even Henry's children were named in memory of his late wife:

Friday 18th April 1862 - at 3 Margaret was born… Margaret Elizabeth Robertson Sandbach is a name combining all that has been dearest to my heart through life - may she grow up worthy of the name she is to bear - may God bless her & keep her for the fold of the good shepherd.

Monday 23rd June 1862 - anniversary of dear Margaret's death 10 years ago - what blessings a kind providence has showered upon me since that time

Roedd yr ailadeiladu yn dasg enfawr ac roedd i ymgorffori twˆr cloc mawreddog. Byddai'r cartref newydd yn dra gwahanol i'r un blaenorol. Yn lle'r cynllun brodorol Cymreig yng nghysgod y bryn gerllaw, byddai hwn yn gartref cwbl gyfoes, â'r cynlluniau'n defnyddio'r technegau adeiladu diweddaraf a defnyddiau o wledydd tramor.

Ailadeiladwyd yr oriel gerfluniau ac oherwydd ei phwysigrwydd, hon oedd rhan gyntaf y tŷ a welwyd gan ymwelwyr wrth nesáu at y brif fynedfa. Siâp octagon oedd ar ystafell fewnol yr oriel fyddai'n coffáu perthynas gymhleth y tri angerddol; y cerfluniau gan Gibson, y comisiwn ar gyfer yr oriel gan Henry; a'r oll dan ysbrydoliaeth Margaret. Oddi fewn y deml hon, gosodwyd penddelwau Henry a Margaret gyferbyn â'i gilydd. Er y gwyddom i Gibson anfon penddelw o'i hunan i Hafodunos, does dim tystiolaeth bod Charlotte wedi'i hanfarwoli yn yr un modd.

Ymgynghorodd Henry'n agos â Gibson ynglŷn ag union leoliad y tŷ a chynllun yr oriel goffa. Roedd Margaret yn bresenoldeb parhaus ym mywydau'r ddau ddyn roedd hi wedi'u caru, yn ystod pob cam o'r adeiladu. Mae dyddiadur Henry'n frith o hanesion sut oedd Margaret ar ei feddwl, flynyddoedd wedi'i marwolaeth. Roedd yn ymweld â'i bedd yn wythnosol, gyda'i wraig Elizabeth. Enwyd plant Henry, hyd yn oed, er cof am ei ddiweddar wraig:

This photograph of Margaret's memorial was sent by Gibson for Henry's approval. Private Collection.

Anfonodd Gibson y ffotograff hwn o gofadail Margaret at Henry er mwyn cael sêl ei fendith arno. Casgliad Preifat.

139

Roedd Gibson yn ŵr prysur iawn gan ei fod bellach yn gerflunydd dethol i'r teulu brenhinol. Er hynny, parhaodd ei gyswllt agos â'r datblygiadau yn Hafodunos, cartref bendigaid Margaret.

Cofnododd ymwelydd cyfoes â Hafodunos yr olwg oedd arno yn fuan wedi cwblhau'r gwelliannau:

Gibson was kept very busy as he had now become the favoured sculptor of the royal family. Nevertheless, he remained closely involved with developments at Margaret's blessed Hafodunos.

A contemporary visitor to Hafodunos records how the house looked shortly after its completion:

'The hall stands on a terrace overlooking a most charming glen, where tulip-trees, great magnolias, hemlocks, and other pines from America mix with native oaks and beeches; where ferns from all parts of Great Britain, Ireland, Switzerland, and New Zealand grow with curious hardy plants from the Continent, and a winding walk leads to the old kitchen-gardens, with their clipped yew-hedges. The interior of the house is in exquisite taste; no paint is allowed, the woodwork and the furniture being of pitch-pine, red cedar, or dark buace from Demerara, whilst the capitals of the columns leading to and on the grand staircase are deftly carved with roses, lilies, snow-drops, and other British flowers.

The first Mrs. Sandbach was a poetess… Her portrait, finely and classically chiselled full-length in bas-relief by Gibson, adorns the vestibule to the room of statuary. This is specially devoted to the works of the same great sculptor and Royal Academician, and contains the fine group of 'The Hunter and his Dog,' the 'Aurora,' together with the busts and medallions of the Sandbach family…

I feel myself once more with the kind owners of Hafodunos in the autumn of 1866. Agreeable county neighbours drive over for afternoon tea; and in the drawing-room, opening on to the terrace, gay with masses of sweet-scented flowers, a noted Welsh painter, quiet, elderly Penry Williams, very modestly exhibits his portfolio of charming Italian landscapes and figures.'[6]

[6] Mary Howitt, Mary Howitt: Volume 2: An Autobiography, p.178–180.

Even after Hafodunos was completed, Margaret's memory raged on in Henry's heart and mind, frequently rereading Margaret's journals and letters and leaving flowers at her grave every Sunday.

Er cwblhau'r gwaith ar Hafodunos, roedd y cof am Margaret yn fyw ym meddwl a chalon Henry. Byddai'n ailddarllen ei dyddiaduron a'i llythyrau drosodd a thro, a gosod blodau ar ei bedd pob Sul.

The newly completed Hafodunos, dated June 5th 1865. National Library of Wales.
Yr Hafodunos newydd orffenedig, dyddiedig 5 Mehefin 1865. Llyfrgell Genedlaethol Cymru.

The Soul

The immortal Soul!
Where is its dwelling place?
Where doth it find a rest
In the wide fields of space?
That ever-burning lamp of light and love
Lit by Omnipotence in realms above!

The immortal Soul!
It dwelleth every where!
Its brightest light is shed
Upon the hour of prayer;
Unseen yet beautiful, we feel it nigh,
The spark of heavenly fire that cannot die.

The immortal Soul!
We catch its radiant gleam,
In the sweet eyes that throw
On ours their tender beam;
And in their glance, its clear and magic spell
A moment pauses, in those depths to dwell.

The immortal Soul!
It is the child of heaven;
A pure and blessed life
Unto our keeping given:
Life within life — the deathless and the free,
The link that binds us to eternity!

*Suffer the little children to come unto me, and forbid them
not; for of such is the kingdom of God.*

Mark X, XIV.

*Engraving of Gibson's design for Christ Blessing the Little Children, contained within
Imitations of Drawings by John Gibson. Private Collection.*

*Ysgythriad o gynllun Gibson ar gyfer Christ Blessing the Little Children, sydd yn Imitations
of Drawings gan John Gibson. Casgliad Preifat.*

The sight of the billiard table in the sculpture room which one suspects would at one time have been almost hallowed ground, speaks of the fleeting nature of our lives, where the sacred of one generation very quickly becomes the old hat nuisance of the next. Time moves on very rapidly, even in this remote corner of Wales.

The sculpture gallery at Hafodunos, conceived as a memorial to Margaret, contained a collection which remained intact until 1969. The Sandbach sculptures were supposed to have been protected by covenants so that they would always remain at Hafodunos but despite this were sold and dispersed in 1969. Fortunately, most were purchased by the Sandbach family, The Walker Art Gallery and National Museum of Wales.

Mae gweld y bwrdd biliards yn ystafell y cerfluniau, a fyddai ar un adeg bron yn dir sanctaidd, yn adlewyrchu natur fyrhoedlog ein bywyd; mae'r hyn sy'n gysegredig i un genhedlaeth yn prysur fynd yn boendod hen ffasiwn i'r genhedlaeth nesaf. Cyflym yw treigl amser, hyd yn oed yn y llecyn diarffordd hwn o Gymru.

Yn yr oriel a luniwyd fel cofeb i Margaret, roedd y casgliad cerfluniau yn gyflawn hyd at 1969. Roedd cyfamod yn bodoli oedd i ddiogelu y cerfluniau Sandbach a sicrhau nad oeddynt byth i adael Hafodunos. Er hynny cawsant eu gwerthu a'u gwasgaru ym 1969. Yn ffodus, prynwyd y rhan fwyaf gan y teulu Sandbach, Oriel Gelf Walker ac Amgueddfa Genedlaethol Cymru.

Theseus and the Robber, contained within Imitations of Drawings by John Gibson.
Private Collection.

Theseus and the Robber, sydd yn Imitations of Drawings gan John Gibson. Casgliad Preifat.

Acknowledgments / Diolchiadau

Mrs. Ian Mackeson-Sandbach
Antoinette Sandbach AM/AC
Auriol, Ardalyddes / Marchioness of Linlithgow

Justin Albert
Ryan Ashford
Roanne Bardsley
Spencer Beale
Yasmine Boudiaf
Eric Forster
Tom Langford
Ceri Leeder
Giuliana Marenghi
Francesca Morgan
Adam Pollock
Matthew Pollock
Neil Pringle
Phillida Wrigley
Nerys Wynn-Jones

Ffotograffau Tablo / Tableaux Photographs
(tt./pp.0-1, 14-15, 34-35, 48-49, 64-65, 88-89, 106-107, 120-121, 130-131)
© Delweddau gan Manuel Vason mewn cydweithrediad â
Truth Department
© Images by Manuel Vason in collaboration with
Truth Department

Maria Agiomyrgianaki
Angelo Constantinou
Oshi Davies
Tim Dickel
Nick Elphick
William Greenwood
Guto Humphreys
Arwyn & Julie Jones
Rebecca Wyn Jones
Kylie Jonkman
Angharad Matthews
Greg Mothersdale
Maisie Noble
Ben Norey
Michelle Outram
Stephen Peckham
Hermes Pittakos
Michael Tree
Rick Wood
Manuel Vason
Joanna Wright

Cyngor Celfyddydau Cymru / Arts Council of Wales
Llywodraeth Cymru / Welsh Government
Y Loteri Genedlaethol / National Lottery

Ffotograffau o Hafodunos a Chasgliadau Preifat gan
Antonia Dewhurst
Photographs of Hafodunos and Private Collections by
Antonia Dewhurst

Yr Academi Frenhinol / The Royal Academy
Yr Amgueddfa Brydeinig
Amgueddfa Syr Henry Jones Museum
Amgueddfeydd Cenedlaethol Cymru / National
Museums of Wales
Archifdy Powys Record Office
Archifdy Sir y Fflint / Flintshire Record Office
Argraffwyr Craig-Y-Don Printers
CADW
Cyngor Llyfrau Cymru / Welsh Books Council
Llenyddiaeth Cymru / Literature Wales
Llyfrgell Genedlaethol Cymru / The National Library of Wales
Micrographics
Ymddiriedolaeth Cadwraeth Castell Gwrych Castle Preservation
Trust
Yr Oriel Bortreadau Genedlaethol / The National Portrait Gallery
Oriel Gelf Walker Art Gallery
Yr Oriel Genedlaethol / The National Gallery
Yr Ymddiriedolaeth Genedlaethol / The National Trust
Partneriaeth Wledig Conwy Rural Partnership
Prifysgol Caerdydd / Cardiff University